EVD 894T

OP   5-

W9-DAJ-089

THE SOLID GOLD CADILLAC

THE

A COMEDY BY

Howard Teichmann *and*

George S. Kaufman

RANDOM HOUSE · NEW YORK

SOLID GOLD CADILLAC

To
Charles E. Wilson, Robert R. Young
and all the other small stockholders of America

The Solid Gold Cadillac was first presented by Max Gordon at the New Parsons Theatre in Hartford, Connecticut, on October 1, 1953. After the customary vicissitudes—plus a few extra ones—in Washington and Philadelphia, it opened at the Belasco Theatre in New York on November 5, 1954. The cast was as follows:

T. JOHN BLESSINGTON	Geoffrey Lumb
ALFRED METCALFE	Wendell K. Phillips
WARREN GILLIE	Reynolds Evans
CLIFFORD SNELL	Henry Jones
MRS. LAURA PARTRIDGE	Josephine Hull
MISS AMELIA SHOTGRAVEN	Mary Welch
MARK JENKINS	Jack Ruth
MISS L'ARRIERE	Charlotte Van Lein
EDWARD L. McKEEVER	Loring Smith
MISS LOGAN	Vera Fuller Mellish
THE A.P.	Carl Judd
THE U.P.	Al McGranary
I.N.S.	Howard Adelman
A LITTLE OLD LADY	Gloria Maitland

NEWS BROADCASTERS

BILL PARKER	Henry Norell
DWIGHT BROOKFIELD	Mark Allen
ESTELLE EVANS	Lorraine MacMartin

Staged by George S. Kaufman
Settings by Edward Gilbert

The action of the play takes place in New York and Washington.

The recitation by Edward L. McKeever, "Spartacus to the Gladiators," complete with gestures, is the invention of Marc Connelly.

And Fred Allen recorded the narration. . . . Damned comically, too.

THE VOICE
by Fred Allen

If you have seen *The Solid Gold Cadillac* you no doubt remember a sepulchral voice that emerged from the woodwork sporadically and guided the audience through the succession of scenes that made up the play.

The voice was mine. You may wonder why, after being away from the Broadway theatre since 1931 (*Three's a Crowd,* with Clifton Webb and Libby Holman), I returned in this play a vocal nonentity without being permitted to assume dimension during the entire evening.

There is a reason. The authors of *The Solid Gold Cadillac,* Howard Teichmann and George S. Kaufman, lured me to artistic extinction. Before their play went into rehearsal, these gentlemen phoned me and pretended that they had a wrong number. Somehow, this led to a discussion of my plans. I advised Messrs. Teichmann and Kaufman that I only had one plan. It was to perpetuate my survival. I reminded them that for many years I had been hawking laxatives, cigarettes and margarine on radio with great success. Mr. Kaufman hinted darkly that television was slowly ruining radio and if my plan involved survival I had better look to the future. Mr. Teichmann interrupted here and said that my future was assured. He and Mr. Kaufman would bring me back to the theatre in their new play, *The Solid Gold Cadillac.*

The rest is perfidy. These two literate charlatans promised me the star dressing room, billing, and the leading role in the play. I have no dressing room. I get no billing. Instead of the leading role my voice is squeezed through a knothole in the proscenium on cue.

Messrs. Teichmann and Kaufman assured me that the minute *The Solid Gold Cadillac* opened I would be made. The offers would pour in. The play has been running many months. My voice has been heard at every performance. Up to now, I have received two offers. One to haunt a housing project over in Jersey. The other offer is to understudy the Voice of America. If the Voice of America ever contracts laryngitis—I go on.

PREFACE

by *Ralph D. Saylor, General Manager,*
the Western Union Telegraph Company

It is a theatrical custom to send opening-night telegrams to the cast and the authors—sometimes even the ushers and the producers—of plays opening on Broadway. The value of these good-luck messages to the recipients has never been scientifically determined. There are cynics who claim that if on the way into the theatre on the night of a première you strike oil in the lobby—that's luck. Nothing else.

But Western Union does not hold with this viewpoint. Opening nights are always lucky for Western Union. On the opening night of *The Solid Gold Cadillac* more than sixteen hundred orchid-bordered telegrams were delivered at the stage door. Consequently, I consider *The Solid Gold Cadillac* a noteworthy drama, a touching and revealing saga of American home life and ideals. *Grandma's Diary,* where we also delivered sixteen hundred telegrams, was equally good.

PREFACE

by Bernhard Gristede, Gristede Bros., Inc.
Quality Retail Food Merchants for over Half a Century

Since the Messrs. Teichmann and Kaufman are both Gristede customers, our credit manager was naturally very happy at the success of *The Solid Gold Cadillac*. One of our speediest delivery boys had rushed copies of the theatrical reviews to us at the cashier's booth of Store No. 14 (our Times Square shop), where, with beating hearts, we sought the verdict.

A look at the papers told us the story. My brothers and I shook hands all around and toasted our good fortune in a Number Five Size (Large) can of our Grisdale Extra Special Fancy Apricot Juice, Unsweetened. Next morning, Mr. Torquemada, in charge of our Credit Department, at once issued orders putting an end to the leberwurst and Ry-Krisp diet on which the authors had been subsisting for a number of years.

The Kaufmans, I am happy to advise, were and still are customers of our Store No. 98, Madison Avenue and Eighty-fifth Street, RE 4-0200, while the Teichmanns patronize Store No. 12, Lexington Avenue and Seventy-seventh Street, RE 4-0112. I trust I am not being indelicate when I say that prior to the opening of *The Solid Gold Cadillac* we had not received a check from either of them for many months. While I do not wish to imply that

Gristede Bros. had anything to do with the writing of *The Solid Gold Cadillac,* I feel that I am on safe ground in saying that without our help there would have been no play. No playwrights, either.

Both the Kaufman cook, a French countess from the Dijon province, as I understand it, and the Teichmann food-stewer, an Alabamian who keeps within constant reach of a water pitcher filled with gin, proved to be most co-operative with our Accounts Receivable Department. Bills marked LONG OVERDUE were rendered by nightfall and were slipped under the playwrights' filet mignons at dinner that evening.

Within six weeks our lawyers concluded negotiations with the Dramatists' Guild. For the remainder of the New York run we are to get five per cent of the first five thousand dollars, seven and one half per cent of the next two thousand, and ten per cent of everything above ten thousand.

This leaves the authors complete freedom from income tax and unlimited credit at all our stores. Nothing is too good for our customers.

PREFACE

by Hon. Walter P. Abbott
Mayor, Natchez, Miss.

Inaccuracy, friends, that's what's ruining the American theatre today. Just plain, old-fashioned American inaccuracy. People write plays, don't bother to check on things, other people go to see those plays, can't believe a word they hear. Take *The Solid Gold Cadillac*. A lot of talk about the fair city of Natchez in that play. "The Jewel of the Swamps." That's what they call fair Natchez. Now, friends, Natchez is located on a fifty-six-foot bluff overlooking the Mississippi River. No swamps within half a mile of us. Maybe the writers meant Upper Natchez. That's to the north of us. They got swamps, plenty. But if they meant Upper Natchez, why didn't they say so?

Well, if the American theatre wants to go down the sink hole because of inaccuracy, that's their lookout. I don't mind. Besides, they haven't turned out a decent play since Edward Ferber wrote *Showboat*.

PREFACE

by Hon. Robert T. Capeless
Mayor, Pittsfield, Mass.

The high moment of *The Solid Gold Cadillac,* as far as most intelligent people are concerned, comes surprisingly early in the play. In the first quarter, I am certain, of the first act. One of the women on the stage, it doesn't matter which one, turns to another woman who is also on the stage and reads a letter postmarked in the city of Pittsfield, seat of Berkshire County, Massachusetts. This is very interesting. Pittsfield has 56,117 people who can write letters.

It also has excellent power facilities, a strong sewage system, and a fine statue of "The Color Bearer" which, during the tourist season, is disguised by the trees in the park facing West Street. Industries are welcome. Kiwanis meets on Wednesday, Rotary on Thursday.

The climactic letter which brings the audiences of *The Solid Gold Cadillac* to its feet each night concerns itself with a Pittsfield firm called the Apex Electric Clock Company. Actually, there *is* no Apex Electric Clock Company in our city, but what undoubtedly served as the inspiration to the authors was the Terry Clock Company which originally came to Pittsfield from Connecticut in 1880. High taxes probably. In 1886 it was reorganized as the Russell-Jones Clock Company. In 1887, it went out of business. Bankrupt. But this is no reflection on Pittsfield. Nor on my administration, for that matter.

PREFACE
by *A Ticket Speculator*

The Solid Gold Cadillac is a great play. On December 7th, 1953, two nights after the opening, I sold Seats F-26 and 27, with a fine view of Seats E-26 and 27, for eleven dollars apiece, or a clear profit of six dollars a ticket, less tax, which I did not pay. The producer paid the actors, the authors, theatre rental and office expenses. He got four dollars a ticket, or a clean profit of a cent and a quarter a seat.

You will not find a finer fellow anywhere than a theatrical producer.

PREFACE
by a Stagehand

I can't honestly say I like this *Cadillac* show very much. Too much scenery-changing. I been with it a year now and the same thing happens every night. "Spike" Conover, "Big Dutch" Klupferman and me, we're down in the cellar and almost before we know whose deal it is the goddamn buzzer goes and we got to drop everything and trot upstairs and change the scenery. One time I pick up a four-fifty hand in spades—cold in my hand, without the kitty even—and bang! up we got to go and change scenery or something. And matinees, if you're on the phone trying to put down a bet at Belmont or some place, the same thing happens.

Now, *Our Town*—there was a show. No scenery at all, the whole evening. I must of held a dozen four-fifty hands that year, and any number of four hundreds. Stage manager come downstairs, we'd just give him the razzberry and go right on playing. Paydays we'd make them bring us down the money.

How about a revival of *Our Town,* somebody?

ACT ONE

Scene 1

The curtain rises to reveal four overstuffed shirts, each one with a man inside it.

They are seated behind a great directors' table— and, indeed, directors are what they are. For this is a stockholders' meeting, somewhere in downtown New York, and our four directors are on hand strictly in their own interests, and not at all concerned with the welfare of the stockholders. But that can wait, since it is the story of the play.

Then, as they stiffly sit there, a voice comes over the loud-speaker. It comes over in the raspy tone of Mr. Fred Allen, and we trust that the reader, if any, will imagine Mr. Allen's wonderful voice as he reads this narration:

THIS IS A FAIRY STORY—THE STORY OF CINDERELLA AND THE FOUR UGLY CORPORATION DIRECTORS. ONCE UPON A TIME, NOT SO LONG AGO, CINDERELLA WENT DOWN TO WALL STREET, NOT IN A GOLD COACH DRAWN BY SIX WHITE HORSES, BUT IN THE I.R.T. SUBWAY.

(One of the stuffed shirts rises and pounds a gavel. His name is T. JOHN BLESSINGTON, *and he looks it. The other three, from whom we presently will hear, are named* ALFRED METCALFE, WARREN GILLIE, *and* CLIFFORD SNELL. *Not that it matters.)*
(But soft! MR. BLESSINGTON *is speaking.)*

BLESSINGTON

Order, please, order! The meeting will come to order. The fifty-ninth annual meeting of the stockholders is hereby declared in session. Stockholders, that is, of the General Products Corporation of America.

(MR. BLESSINGTON *looks the stockholders over*)

No doubt many of you are surprised to find me acting as chairman of this meeting. No more so than I. My seat has always been Mr. Metcalfe's—that is, where Mr. Metcalfe is *sitting*. However, due to our great and irreplaceable loss—I have naturally, and legally too, I am informed, moved up one notch. Not that I shall ever be able to fill the place left vacant by our beloved Ed McKeever—Big Ed, as he was known to those who loved him.

(*The others look appropriately solemn*)

Edward L. McKeever made this great company what it is today—one of the largest corporations in the United States. In his nineteen years as President and Chairman of the Board he saw your company grow until it now manufactures everything from pins to automobiles, from a nail file to tractors and locomotives. Yes, I can safely say: if General Products doesn't make it, there's no money in it. Now I will call upon your new President—Acting President, I should say, until you make him your new President, who will tell you what your Board of Directors proposes to do to honor our great former leader. . . . Mr. Alfred Metcalfe.

METCALFE

(*The rough-diamond type*)

Thank you, Mr. Blessington. Yes, General Products lost a good man when the President called Ed McKeever to Washington. You all remember what happened down there—I'm sure you read about it in the papers. Before they would give him the job he was forced by the Government to take a profit of three million dollars in General Products stock. But did he hesitate? Only for a week or so. That is why we are sending him this scroll: "To Edward Leon McKeever, slag hauler, furnace feeder, assembly-line worker, foreman, shop supervisor, plant manager, Vice-President, and, for nineteen years, President and Chairman of the Board of the General Products Corporation of America—with the gratitude and affection of labor, management and capital." I just want to add that in the good old days I worked on the slag pile with Ed McKeever, and that nobody ever slung as much slag as Big Ed.

(*A smattering of applause, for no good reason*)

BLESSINGTON

Thank you, Mr. Metcalfe. The chair will entertain a motion to have the scroll duly delivered to Mr. McKeever in Washington.

METCALFE

So moved.

BLESSINGTON

Thank you. Do I hear a second?

GILLIE

Second.

SNELL

(*Indicates a great pile of proxies*)

Voting 750,000 shares by duly authorized proxy, I say aye.

5

BLESSINGTON

Thank you. Opposed? . . . Motion carried by acclamation. . . . And now the next business of the meeting—the report of your Secretary, Mr. Warren Gillie.

GILLIE

(Really *a dull fellow*)

The stockholders will have found on their chairs a little white booklet—

(*He holds one up as example; reads the title*)

—"Compendium of Minutes of Quarterly Meetings of Directors of General Products Corporation." . . . As the stockholders know, the posts of Chairman of the Board and President of the Corporation were both held by Mr. McKeever. In the new alignment, delegation of responsibility is proposed as follows: T. John Blessington, from First Vice-President to Chairman of the Board;

(BLESSINGTON *smiles, fatuously*)

Alfred Metcalfe, from Second Vice-President to President of the company.

(METCALFE *pretends to be embarrassed*)

Clifford Snell, from Treasurer to Administrative Vice-President *and* Treasurer.

(SNELL *grins—a phony if ever there was one*)

Warren Gillie, Secretary, to remain as Secretary. Respectfully submitted, Warren Gillie, Secretary.

(*And he sits, before anyone can throw an egg.*)

BLESSINGTON

(*Rises*)

Thank you, Mr. Gillie. Do I hear a motion to accept Mr. Gillie's report?

6

SNELL

Moved.

METCALFE

Second.

SNELL

(*Right on the job*)

750,000 proxies vote aye.

BLESSINGTON

Opposed? Carried. And now, the report of the man you're really waiting to hear from, your Treasurer, Mr. Clifford Snell.

SNELL

(*We don't have to mince words here—*SNELL *is a plain crook*)

Thank you, Jack.

(*The big smile*)

Well folks, I'm the fellow you either like or dislike. Depending on the size of the dividend check, eh?

(*The other three laugh it up, even if the audience doesn't*)

And here's the report on how we did this year. I'm sure all of you have found it on your chairs, alongside of Mr. Gillie's little booklet. It isn't as compact as Warren's report, but then you can't do things with figures the way you can with words.

(*Another laugh from his associates. Jolly good fellows they*)

Anyhow, suppose you and I kind of thumb through it together. . . . Let's see. Page 11—just as one example. Page 11. Assets—26 billion, one million, seven hundred and ninety-two thousand, eight hundred and ninety-one dollars and seventy-two cents. Now, I think that's pretty good, don't you?

(*The big grin again. Here is a fellow to avoid even in a* light *alley.*)

BLESSINGTON

Fine, Clifford. Just fine.

GILLIE

Fine!

SNELL

Page 32. Inventory. Starts on Page 32, runs to Page 57, and you'll find a pretty complete list there, from the raw stock in our Allegheny steel plant to the little cellophane price tags in our Denver merchandising rooms.

(*Idly flipping pages*)

Pages 161, 162, all the way up to 170—gross profits, net gains, interest charges, dividend payments, and the like . . . Well, folks, that's the story. I might add that now, at long last, since we finally have an administration in Washington that understands business—our dividend this quarter will be slightly smaller. Of course, that's only temporary. . . .

(*He sits, but bounces up again*)

The smaller dividend will be temporary, I mean, not the administration in Washington.

(*And he is finished.*)

BLESSINGTON

Thank you, Mr. Snell. Now will anyone move for the adoption of Mr. Snell's report?

METCALFE

(*Fast as hell*)

Moved.

GILLIE

(*Even faster than hell*)

Second.

SNELL

(*Much faster than hell*)

Proxies vote aye.

BLESSINGTON

It's been moved and seconded that the report of the Treasurer, Mr. Clifford Snell, be unanimously adopted. All those in favor—Yes, Madam?

(*A dumpy little woman has got to her feet. A real charmer, but tough. Having got up, she is really never going to sit down again till the show is over*)

THE WOMAN

Oh! Well, I'm sorry—it's nothing, really.

BLESSINGTON

Then you don't wish the chair to recognize you?

THE WOMAN

(*Looking around a little uncertainly*)

The—chair?

BLESSINGTON

I am the chair, Madame.

THE WOMAN

Oh. I didn't quite—

BLESSINGTON

Do you wish the chair to recognize you?

THE WOMAN

I *did* have something I wanted to ask, but—

BLESSINGTON

Certainly, Madame. What was it you wanted to know?

THE WOMAN

Well, it's not really something I want to know, exactly—
it's—kind of something I don't like.

SNELL

Can't we get ahead with this, Jack?

BLESSINGTON

Something you don't like? What is it?

THE WOMAN

Well, it's—this.
(*She holds up the blue book.*)

BLESSINGTON

You don't like Mr. Snell's report? All of it?

THE WOMAN

No, I don't mean all of it. I—I like the color.

SNELL

Isn't this a little ridiculous?

THE WOMAN

I'm sorry, I—I've never attended a stockholders' meeting before. Maybe I'd better sit down.

BLESSINGTON

Just as you wish, Madame.

THE WOMAN

Thank you.

BLESSINGTON

Now, there is a motion—

THE WOMAN

On the other hand—it says here that the salary for the Chairman of the Board next year will be $175,000.
(*Gossipy*)
Tell me—is that true?

BLESSINGTON

Well—uh—wherever did you get a notion like that, Miss —uh—

THE WOMAN

Mrs. Mrs. Partridge. It's on Page 96. Right here.

BLESSINGTON

I see. Uh—Mr. Snell, as Treasurer, would you care to answer that question?

SNELL

(*Brightly*)

Yes, indeed! Happy to oblige . . . The—uh—could I hear the question again, please?

MRS. PARTRIDGE

I don't want anyone to think I'm nosy, but is it true that the Chairman will get $175,000 next year? It seems such a lot of money.

SNELL

Why—Madam. In a company of this size that is not considered a large salary. Not a large salary at all. I believe that answers the question.

(*And pretty smug he is.*)

BLESSINGTON

Yes. There is a motion—

MRS. PARTRIDGE

(*Not one to give up*)

Well, would I be just awful if I asked another question? What does the Chairman of the Board do?

SNELL

My dear lady, as an attorney I can assure you that the office of Chairman of the Board is one prescribed by law. New York State Corporation Code, Section 23. We have very little to say about it—we're just obeying the law.

MRS. PARTRIDGE

Oh, I'm sure of that. Only—what does he do?

BLESSINGTON
(The four look at each other. This is really a tough one)
He presides over the board. The Chairman of the Board presides over the board of directors.

MRS. PARTRIDGE
Now I understand. Thank you so much.

(The stuffed shirts breathe easier.)

BLESSINGTON
Not at all. We are always happy to—

MRS. PARTRIDGE
How often does he do that?

BLESSINGTON
I beg your pardon?

MRS. PARTRIDGE
How often does he preside over the board?

BLESSINGTON
(Damned if he knows)
Why—uh—how often *is* that, Mr. Gillie?

GILLIE
(With his dreams)
How's that?

BLESSINGTON
How often does the Board meet?

13

GILLIE

Why—four times a year, isn't it?
(*Firmly, to* MRS. PARTRIDGE)
Four times every year.

SNELL

That is also prescribed by law.

MRS. PARTRIDGE

Now I know I'm asking a lot of questions, but—how long do the meetings last?

BLESSINGTON

(*Walking right into it*)
Oh, several hours. At least several hours.

MRS. PARTRIDGE

Two hours, would you say?

BLESSINGTON

Yes. Yes, indeed. And then there's the annual stockholders' meeting.

MRS. PARTRIDGE

So that makes five times?

SNELL

Excuse me, Jack . . . Uh—Mrs. Partridge—that's right, Partridge?

MRS. PARTRIDGE

Yes, sir.

SNELL

(*As to a child*)
You understand this is a stockholders' meeting?

MRS. PARTRIDGE

Oh, yes.

SNELL

You *are* a—stockholder?

MRS. PARTRIDGE

Oh yes. I have ten shares. I've had them for a long time, only I've never come to a meeting before.

SNELL

Your full name and address, Mrs. uh—
(*He motions to* GILLIE *to confirm.*)

MRS. PARTRIDGE

Mrs. Laura Partridge, 226-a 18th St., Jackson Heights, Long Island.

GILLIE

(*Looks in the book*)
Paddington, Partridge . . .
(*Reluctantly*)
Mrs. Laura Partridge. Ten shares, stock certificate No. 18973635.

(*The boys are anything but pleased at this.*)

MRS. PARTRIDGE

Yes. I haven't got it with me. It's in my top bureau drawer.

SNELL

(*Escorting her toward her chair*)
Now we have many points on the agenda, so—

MRS. PARTRIDGE
(*Not to be silenced*)
Well, five meetings a year—that's ten hours in all—you mean he gets $175,000 for just working ten hours?

SNELL
(*He can answer that—he* thinks)
Not at all. The Chairman of the Board must be intimately conversant with every detail of the company at all times—that requires constant study, brain work.

BLESSINGTON
It's a big job, Mrs. Partridge—a very big job. Responsibilities to the company, to the nation, and, in these times, to the world.

MRS. PARTRIDGE
Ye-es . . . Still—$175,000. And you're going to get $100,-000, Mr. Snell.

SNELL
(*Blandly*)
And don't you think I'm worth $100,000, Mrs. Partridge?

MRS. PARTRIDGE
Not if we can get somebody for less.
(*Well,* SNELL *asked for it*)
You see, the reason I came here today, it says it's a good day to attend to financial matters.

BLESSINGTON
I beg your pardon?

MRS. PARTRIDGE
My horoscope. I'm Leo the Lion. It says:

(*She reads*)
"Cultivate friends and attend to financial matters."

SNELL

BLESSINGTON
(*He hadn't figured on* this)
I see.

SNELL
Isn't there a motion before the house?

MRS. PARTRIDGE
Mind you, I don't really pay much attention to it. Now that I'm here I'm much more interested in the salaries.

BLESSINGTON
(*So sweet*)
And we want you to be. Now what is it you would like to know?

MRS. PARTRIDGE
Well, it says you used to get $75,000 and now it's going to be $175,000—that's $100,000 more—now, how much did *you* used to get, Mr. Snell?

SNELL
(*Let's not go into* that)
Madame, that is not the point.

MRS. PARTRIDGE
Goodness, I know it isn't, but let's add up, just for fun. Shall we? May I borrow your pencil?—Thank you.
(*She takes* SNELL's *pencil out of his pocket*)
Now, how much did you say you used to get, Mr. Snell?

17

SNELL

(What *a nuisance!*)
You'll find everything in the report. I don't recall that—

MRS. PARTRIDGE

Oh, here it is. Fifty thousand dollars. Of course, to the ordinary person, fifty thousand dollars—gracious!

SNELL

(*A desperate look to* BLESSINGTON)
This seems to me hardly a matter for—

MRS. PARTRIDGE

Well, I don't mean to be a nuisance, but—can just anybody make a motion?

BLESSINGTON

Certainly, Madame.

MRS. PARTRIDGE

Oh, good! Well, I move the salaries are too big.

(*Having tossed this bombshell, she sits down*)

BLESSINGTON

(*Trapped*)
It is not quite the proper form for a motion, Mrs. Partridge—however, if someone seconds it—do I hear a second to Mrs. Partridge's motion?

(*There is no response for a moment, but then it comes.*)

MRS. PARTRIDGE

(*Brightly*)
I second it.

SNELL

Madame, you cannot second your own motion.

MRS. PARTRIDGE

Why not? I'm for it.

SNELL

It's a matter of parliamentary law.

MRS. PARTRIDGE

I don't care what they do in Parliament—I think the salaries are too big, and that some of us here ought to form a stockholders' committee.

BLESSINGTON

   (*Stunned*)
A committee?

GILLIE

Committee?
   (*There is an impromptu conference at the table.*)

MRS. PARTRIDGE

To look into the salaries of our company's directors. And until we come back with our report—

SNELL .

I object, Mr. Chairman!

METCALFE

Mrs. Partridge, I don't think this is the time—

MRS. PARTRIDGE

Because I've known a lot of directors and they didn't get anything like that. So if the committee finds—

BLESSINGTON

(*A panicky look at his fellows*)

Mrs. Partridge, the chair has decided not to act on the matter of salaries today. The meeting is adjourned, if someone will so move.

SNELL

(*Lightning-fast*)

Moved.

METCALFE

Second.

BLESSINGTON

It's moved and seconded that we adjourn—opposed? Carried.

(*Bangs gavel, thank God that's over*)

The meeting is adjourned. The meeting is adjourned for six weeks.

MRS. PARTRIDGE

Six weeks! I can come.

BLESSINGTON

That's splendid!

(*But we doubt if he means it. In fact, a council of war is taking place among our four boy friends. Something has to be done.* MR. BLESSINGTON, *accordingly, takes the bull by the horns*)

Madame, would you remain a moment, please?

MRS. PARTRIDGE

Me?

BLESSINGTON

If you please. I'd like to talk to you a moment.

MRS. PARTRIDGE

You're going to scold me. I know. I've behaved badly.

BLESSINGTON

Not at all. You showed very fine business sense.

METCALFE

(*Coming through for a pal*)

Very fine.

MRS. PARTRIDGE

I did?

BLESSINGTON

You did indeed. So much so that—

(*He is feeling his way, with an eye on his associates*)

—I wonder if we shouldn't take advantage of your business abilities—I mean, here at General Products. How would you like to come to work with us here?

MRS. PARTRIDGE

What kind of work?

BLESSINGTON

Well, I don't know exactly. But you seem to have a keen insight into business affairs. I'm sure you can be of aid to us.

MRS. PARTRIDGE

Oh, but I've never worked in my life, Mr. Blessington. I'm an actress.

BLESSINGTON

(*With feigned interest*)

An actress!

SNELL

Well, well!

METCALFE

An actress! Would I—would I have seen you on the stage?

MRS. PARTRIDGE

Well, I don't know—did you see *Ah, Wilderness*?

BLESSINGTON

Ah, Wilderness . . . I believe so. You were the—uh—

MRS. PARTRIDGE

I was one of the women.

BLESSINGTON

Oh, yes.

METCALFE

I think I remember. Very good. Yes.

BLESSINGTON

You're not acting in a play now?

MRS. PARTRIDGE

No, I'm not.

BLESSINGTON

Then would you be free to associate yourself with us?

SNELL

Are you sure Mrs. Partridge wants to come with us, Jack? Maybe she wouldn't like it.

MRS. PARTRIDGE

Oh, I'd love it.
(*Down to business*)
What about salary?

BLESSINGTON

A *hundred dollars,* Mrs. Partridge. A *hundred dollars a week.* How's *that?*

MRS. PARTRIDGE

Well, I got a hundred and a quarter from the Theatre Guild.

BLESSINGTON

Well, Mrs. Partridge, we *want* you *here* with *us.* So what would you say to a hundred and fifty?

MRS. PARTRIDGE

A hundred and fifty. Yes, that would be better.

BLESSINGTON

Then it's all settled. Let's say you report to me—that's on the thirty-fifth floor—Monday morning at nine o'clock?

MRS. PARTRIDGE

(What *an idea*)
Nine o'clock!

BLESSINGTON

Would you rather come at some other hour?

MRS. PARTRIDGE

Well, in the theatre we don't generally start until eleven.

BLESSINGTON

Eleven would be quite agreeable. That's Monday morning at eleven.

MRS. PARTRIDGE

Yes, that's fine.
(*Going through her astrology book*)
Wait a minute. I can't start Monday. It's a bad day for me to go out—see?

BLESSINGTON

Tuesday then?

MRS. PARTRIDGE

Tuesday . . .
(*Consulting her book*)
"Start new enterprises"—it's perfect. And it's the 17th—that's my lucky number—17. . . . You know, you ought to get one of these.

BLESSINGTON

Well, maybe we can use yours.

MRS. PARTRIDGE

Certainly. Because whoever picked the day for this meeting—
(*She beams at them*)
—well, it wasn't a very good time for you, was it?

And that is Scene 1

The Narrator

SO CINDERELLA WENT TO WORK FOR THE FOUR UGLY CORPO-
RATION DIRECTORS AT $150 A WEEK. BUT IN ONE RESPECT,
CINDERELLA WAS JUST LIKE THE REST OF US. THEY SOAKED
HER FOR WITHHOLDING TAX, WORKMEN'S COMPENSATION
TAX, PERSONAL PROPERTY TAX, STATE INCOME TAX, CITY TAX,
COUNTY TAX, UNEMPLOYMENT TAX, HOSPITALIZATION TAX,
SOCIAL SECURITY TAX, AND SOCIAL INSECURITY TAX.

Scene 2

An almost pathetically small office. A desk and two chairs, bookcase and hat rack.

CLIFFORD SNELL *and a severely tailored secretary are talking together.*

SNELL

I want to emphasize one thing, Miss Shotgraven. Mrs. Partridge's activities on behalf of the company must be very slight. It is your job to see that she does little or nothing. Is that clear?

MISS SHOTGRAVEN

You'll find me most co-operative, Mr. Snell.

SNELL

Then we understand each other. You will report to me if anything unusual happens.

MISS SHOTGRAVEN

Yes, sir. May I ask how long Mrs. Partridge will be with us?

(BLESSINGTON *enters with* MRS. PARTRIDGE)

BLESSINGTON

Yes, here we are. You remember Mr. Snell of course!

26

MRS. PARTRIDGE

Yes, indeed.

SNELL

Good morning, Mrs. Partridge! This is your secretary, Miss Shotgraven.

MISS SHOTGRAVEN

How do you do, Mrs. Partridge?

MRS. PARTRIDGE

Good morning, dear . . . My, the business world is fascinating. I know I'm going to love it. Only you gentlemen haven't told me yet just what I'm supposed to do.

BLESSINGTON

Mrs. Partridge, we are going to make you Director of Stockholder Relations.

MRS. PARTRIDGE

How nice!

BLESSINGTON

I hoped you'd like it.

MRS. PARTRIDGE

What is it?

BLESSINGTON

Why—uh—we have a great many stockholders, Mrs. Partridge—many of them women, like yourself, who own just a few shares—and it will be your job to keep them happy, make friends for the company.

MRS. PARTRIDGE

I see. Will they be coming in?

BLESSINGTON

No, no.

SNELL

We hope not.

BLESSINGTON

But occasionally we receive letters from them, and—uh—when we do receive such letters, they will be turned over to you to answer.

MRS. PARTRIDGE

And that's all I'm to do?

BLESSINGTON

That's quite a lot, Mrs. Partridge. We have more than four million stockholders.

MRS. PARTRIDGE

My!

SNELL

Jack, the meeting on short-term debentures is set for 11:20.

BLESSINGTON

Right! Good luck, Mrs. Partridge, and we're so pleased to have you with us.

MRS. PARTRIDGE

Thank you. Good-bye.

BLESSINGTON

Good-bye.

SNELL

Good-bye.
(*The two men go.*)

MRS. PARTRIDGE
(*Right on the job*)
How soon is lunch?

MISS SHOTGRAVEN
How's that?

MRS. PARTRIDGE
(*Discovers a dictaphone on her desk*)
What's that?

MISS SHOTGRAVEN
Your dictaphone. On evenings that you work late, and choose not to keep me on overtime, you use that for your dictation. Then I transcribe the following morning.

MRS. PARTRIDGE
Oh, I've heard of these. Those rich radio actors have them.

MISS SHOTGRAVEN
Simply pick up the microphone and press that button. That's right. Do you have something to say?

MRS. PARTRIDGE
I don't know.
(*A thoughtful pause; then into the machine*)
"The quality of mercy is not strained. It droppeth as—"

(*A stocky but handsome young man enters—shirt-sleeved, and carrying a clipboard to which are affixed a stack of papers. Also a thick, heavy pencil*)

29

THE YOUNG MAN
(*Businesslike as hell*)
Partridge?

MISS SHOTGRAVEN
(*With dignity*)
This is Mrs. Partridge's office.

THE YOUNG MAN
Jenkins, Incoming Mail . . . How do you spell that name?

MRS. PARTRIDGE
P - a - r - t —

MISS SHOTGRAVEN
(*Taking it away from her*)
R - i - d - g - e.

JENKINS
First name?

MRS. PARTRIDGE
Laura.

MISS SHOTGRAVEN
(*A look at her*)
Laura.

JENKINS
Yours or hers?

MISS SHOTGRAVEN
Mrs. Laura Partridge.

JENKINS
Okay! Room 2762.
(*He makes a quick note*)
Any mail comes, you'll get it.
(*He goes.*)

MISS SHOTGRAVEN

(*Pulling herself together. The young man has obviously made an impression*)

Shall we begin?

MRS. PARTRIDGE

Yes . . . Begin what?

MISS SHOTGRAVEN

Begin work.

MRS. PARTRIDGE

Oh yes. Where are the letters from the stockholders?

MISS SHOTGRAVEN

I haven't seen any, Mrs. Partridge.

MRS. PARTRIDGE

But Mr. Blessington just said—

MISS SHOTGRAVEN

He said if any should come in.

MRS. PARTRIDGE

Oh! Then what do we do? Just wait?

MISS SHOTGRAVEN

Your schedule is clear until 11:55. All executives are required in the main lobby at 11:55 for the unveiling of a bust of Mr. McKeever.

MRS. PARTRIDGE

Well, that'll be interesting.

(*Studies* MISS SHOTGRAVEN *a second*)

Do you always wear your hair that way, dear?

MISS SHOTGRAVEN

I do.

MRS. PARTRIDGE

There's a little hairdresser on 53rd Street . . .

MISS SHOTGRAVEN

(*Briskly*)

Please, Mrs. Partridge. Not during business hours.

MRS. PARTRIDGE

I'm sorry.

(MR. GILLIE *comes in—all business.*)

GILLIE

Good morning, Mrs. Partridge.

MRS. PARTRIDGE

Good morning, Mr. Gillie.

GILLIE

(*Pompously*)

Mrs. Partridge, we're giving a dinner next week to honor Mr. Blessington on his promotion to Chairman of the Board, and we'd be so pleased if you would attend. Tickets are twenty-five dollars.

MRS. PARTRIDGE

Twenty-five dollars! What are you going to have for dinner?

GILLIE

Mrs. Partridge, that is not the point.

MRS. PARTRIDGE

The hell it isn't!

(MR. GILLIE *gets out of there fast—happy to escape.*)

MRS. PARTRIDGE
(*To* MISS SHOTGRAVEN)
Now, where were we?

MISS SHOTGRAVEN

You were about to dictate.

MRS. PARTRIDGE

Yes.
(*But unable to leave the subject*)
Do you have any beaus? I suppose you have a lot of beaus.
Tell me about them.

MISS SHOTGRAVEN

Please, Mrs. Partridge, I must insist upon a business relationship. Either you must dictate or I shall have to leave the office.

MRS. PARTRIDGE

I'm so sorry. Now let me see . . . Whom can I—Oh, I know. "Dear Eddie:"

MISS SHOTGRAVEN

But whom is it going to?

MRS. PARTRIDGE

To Eddie.

MISS SHOTGRAVEN

But first you have to give me his full name and address,
and then you can begin "Dear Eddie."

MRS. PARTRIDGE

But that's all the name he has—Eddie—and I don't know
his address.

MISS SHOTGRAVEN

Then how will it reach him?

MRS. PARTRIDGE

I'll just put it in the milk bottle. "Dear Eddie. Please do
not leave the half pint of cream every morning, as I will
not be home for lunch any more. So just leave it every
other day. Thank you. Mrs. Partridge."
(*The telephone rings. She quickly picks up the receiver*)
Hello.

MISS SHOTGRAVEN

(*Horrified*)
Mrs. Partridge!
(*She takes the receiver from her*)
Mrs. Partridge's secretary speaking . . . Who wants to
speak to Mrs. Partridge? . . . One moment please—I'll
see if she is in.

MRS. PARTRIDGE

I'm in.

MISS SHOTGRAVEN

(*Refusing to give her the phone*)
What does he want to talk to Mrs. Partridge about?

MRS. PARTRIDGE

I haven't anything to do—isn't it all right if I talk to him?

MISS SHOTGRAVEN

(*Covering phone*)

Not to a theatrical agent, Mrs. Partridge.

MRS. PARTRIDGE

A theatrical agent!

(*Takes phone from her*)

Who's this—Tom Lynch? . . . How on earth did you find me? . . . Oh, yes, my answering service . . . Yes, I *am* working again . . . No, I've quit the theatre . . . $150 a week . . . Well, I don't see why you should get 10 percent of *that,* Tom. . . . All right, *take* me off your list! You haven't got me a job in six years, not even modeling!

(*Hangs up*)

MISS SHOTGRAVEN

(*A new respect*)

Why, Mrs. Partridge! I didn't know you'd been in the theatre.

MRS. PARTRIDGE

(*Quite calmly*)

Really, dear?

MISS SHOTGRAVEN

It must have been terribly exciting! Especially in the old days!

MRS. PARTRIDGE

The old days, Miss Shotgraven, were strictly n.g. That means no good. Rehearse for ten weeks without pay, go on the road and the company manager would make off with the receipts. That happened to me once. And the worst of it was that I was married to him. That was the last time I saw him, except at the funeral. Poor Harry. Now, Miss—uh—what's that name of yours again?

MISS SHOTGRAVEN

Shotgraven. Amelia Shotgraven.

MRS. PARTRIDGE
(*With new authority*)
Oh, I'd change that if I were you.

MISS SHOTGRAVEN

Tell me some more of your experiences when you were acting.

MRS. PARTRIDGE

Not during business hours, Miss Shotgraven.

MISS SHOTGRAVEN
(*Back into her shell*)
Quite right. Sorry.

MRS. PARTRIDGE

Now, Miss Shotgraven, is there any way of finding out some of the stockholders' names?

MISS SHOTGRAVEN

Well, there's the—uh—stockholders' directory.

MRS. PARTRIDGE

Would you bring it to me, please?
(MISS SHOTGRAVEN *does so*)
Thank you.

MISS SHOTGRAVEN

This is somewhat irregular, Mrs. Partridge.

MRS. PARTRIDGE

Alabama, Arizona, Arkansas. I don't want anybody from
Arkansas. We starved to death there. . . . Louisiana,
Maine, Maryland. We did good business in Maryland.
. . . Take a letter, Miss Shotgraven.

MISS SHOTGRAVEN

A letter, Mrs. Partridge?

MRS. PARTRIDGE

Yes.

MISS SHOTGRAVEN

To a stockholder?

MRS. PARTRIDGE

Mr. Blessington told me to make friends. . . . Ready?

MISS SHOTGRAVEN

(*Stiffly*)
Yes, Mrs. Partridge.

MRS. PARTRIDGE

Mrs. Emily Woodbury—that's a friendly name, don't you
think? Two-sixteen Fremont Street, Hagerstown, Mary-

37

land. Twenty-five shares. That's not too many—twenty-five—so she can't be rich. "Dear Mrs. Woodbury: My name is Laura Partridge, and I am a woman just like yourself, except that you probably have a husband and children, and I haven't. However, I am helping out here at General Products these days—just making suggestions. But I'm sure you also have some suggestions you would like to make—just little homey ones, about their stoves or sewing machines and things—or maybe you would like them to invent something. Because we have a lot of inventors here, and they haven't anything to do except invent. Hoping to hear from you soon" . . . Do you have all that written down, dear?

MISS SHOTGRAVEN

Yes, Mrs. Partridge.

MRS. PARTRIDGE

Well, you typewrite it out, and I'll go through the book for more places and names that sound good.

MISS SHOTGRAVEN

More?

MRS. PARTRIDGE

Now—Massachusetts, Minnesota, Mississippi . . .
(*She is turning pages of the directory.*)

The Curtains Close

The Narrator

MEANWHILE THE FOUR UGLY CORPORATION DIRECTORS WERE HAVING A WONDERFUL TIME. THEY WERE RUNNING THE COMPANY ALL OVER THE PLACE. TWICE A DAY THEY WATERED THE STOCK, TO KEEP IT FRESH. AND EVERY SATURDAY THEY TOOK A LONG PAIR OF GARDEN SHEARS AND TRIMMED THE DIVIDEND. ALL IN ALL, YOU WOULD NOT FIND A NICER BUNCH OF FELLOWS OUTSIDE OF A POLICE LINE-UP.

Scene 3

The big office.
Three of the governing board of four are present
—METCALFE, BLESSINGTON *and* SNELL.
They are studiously regarding a beautiful blonde
in a skimpy bathing suit—a luscious dame who is
obviously there on business, but still luscious. She
is holding a pose—about to dive. BLESSINGTON *cir-*
cles around her, appraisingly.

BLESSINGTON

Excellent, Miss L'Arriere. Excellent. . . . All right with
you boys?

METCALFE

(*A grunt*)
All right.
(SNELL *grunts an assent and then* GILLIE *enters.*
Stops short on seeing the girl)

GILLIE

What's this?

BLESSINGTON

Advertising Department. She's a model. She's from the
advertising department.

GILLIE

We're not making bathing suits, are we?

40

BLESSINGTON

It's not for bathing suits, Warren. It's for—what is it again, Miss L'Arriere? What's the slogan?

MISS L'ARRIERE

(*One of those awful voices*)

"I had my swimming pool dug by a General Products steam shovel."

BLESSINGTON

There you are—it's for steam shovels.

GILLIE

Oh! Then why don't they use a steam shovel?

BLESSINGTON

Because nobody would want to look at a steam shovel. . . . All right, Miss L'Arriere.

MISS L'ARRIERE

Thank you, Mr. Blessington.

(*She goes.*)

(METCALFE *goes to work at a little work table, sanding a piece of wood at an electrically run sand-papering machine. It makes a terrific* whirr *as he works it.*)

GILLIE

I've just been on the phone with Mr. McKeever down in Washington.

SNELL

What?

GILLIE

I say I've just been talking to Mr. McKeever on the phone.

SNELL

(*Unable to hear above the whirr*)
Stop that thing a minute, will you, Al?
(METCALFE *shuts off the machine*)
What are you doing anyhow?

METCALFE

I'm making a chair leg.

SNELL

I wish you wouldn't do it when we're talking.

METCALFE

Look! You've got your hobbies, I've got mine.

SNELL

(*Ever the logician*)
Yes, but my hobbies don't irritate me.

METCALFE

Okay—don't get sore.

SNELL

(*Turns to* GILLIE)
What'd he say?

GILLIE

Who?

SNELL

McKeever, of course. What'd he *say*?

GILLIE

Nothing in particular.

SNELL

You mean you didn't take it up with him?

GILLIE

No.

SNELL

Why not? . . . Do you men realize we haven't had a single Government order since McKeever took that job?

BLESSINGTON

He's just leaning over backwards, that's all.

SNELL

Do you know what corporate earnings are going to look like this year?

METCALFE

Ed'll come through for us. I've known Ed for thirty years.

SNELL

Last December our gross dealings with the Government came to a hundred million dollars. That's before Mc-Keever went down there. Since then, nothing.

GILLIE

(*Pulling a trick pen from his pocket*)
Say, fellows, did I show you this gadget? Picked it up in a novelty store. It's a pen that lights up, so that you can write in the dark. . . . See?

BLESSINGTON

Is that what you do in the dark?

GILLIE

Well, I thought if you all liked it we might buy the patent and manufacture it ourselves.

(MISS L'ARRIERE *returns, dressed now in a feminine*

version of a railroad engineer's cap, gauntlets, and little else. She carries an idealized oil can.)

BLESSINGTON
(*Hurrying to her*)
Yes?—What's the slogan this time, Miss L'Arriere?

MISS L'ARRIERE
"My train is pulled by a General Products Diesel."

BLESSINGTON
Oh, yes . . . Excellent!

METCALFE
(*Studying the ensemble*)
The neck ain't right.

BLESSINGTON
What?

METCALFE
The neck ain't right.

BLESSINGTON
What's the matter with her neck?

METCALFE
Not *hers*. The oil can's.

BLESSINGTON
Oh.

METCALFE
Ought to be straight. A Diesel oil can has a straight neck.

BLESSINGTON

(*Angrily*)

I'll send a memo to Wilcox on it.

METCALFE

Okay.

BLESSINGTON

(*Now very sweet*)

All right, Miss L'Arriere.

MISS L'ARRIERE

Thank you, Mr. Blessington.
(*She goes.*)

GILLIE

Say! I have something to tell you fellows.

SNELL

About McKeever?

GILLIE

No! You know that little Apex Company? Massachusetts. We put them into bankruptcy yesterday.

BLESSINGTON

Splendid, Warren!

METCALFE

What's the Apex Company?

GILLIE

Apex Electric Clock Company. Pittsfield, Massachusetts. I found out we were taking a trimming from some little clock manufacturer up in New England—remember?

SNELL

Yes, yes.

GILLIE

Well, we aren't taking it from now on.

METCALFE

We buy 'em out?

GILLIE

Not me! I stole a leaf out of Mr. McKeever's book—
forced 'em out. Undersold them by 50 per cent and kept
on doing it until they cried "Uncle!" So yesterday, under
they went.

BLESSINGTON

Marvelous, Warren!

GILLIE

(*Modestly*)
Well, it'll look good in the annual report.

METCALFE

I don't know. Think we should have done that?

BLESSINGTON

Free enterprise, Al.

METCALFE

(*Returns to his machine*)
Just the same, I can't forget that we were a little company
once.
(*Turns on his machine*)

SNELL

Now if you fellows are finished there's something *I* want
to take up.

46

METCALFE
(*Turns off his machine*)
I just don't like the idea of putting little companies out of business.

SNELL
You know something, Al? You always turn that thing off when *you* talk, so that you can hear what *you're* going to say.

METCALFE
Okay, it's off. Now what is it?

SNELL
Well, it's that pheasant woman.

BLESSINGTON
Who?

SNELL
Pheasant, Partridge, whatever her name is.

BLESSINGTON
What about her? It's only three weeks—can't let her go yet.

SNELL
I'll tell you what about her. She's costing us ninety-five dollars a week for postage, that's what about her.
(GILLIE *meanwhile has gone to the light switch and now plunges the room into darkness. He holds up the lighted pen triumphantly.*)

GILLIE
See what I mean!?

SNELL

Oh, for God's sake, Warren!

GILLIE

(*Puts on the lights*)
How do you know she's costing us all that postage?

SNELL

I know because I got the figures from the mail room. She's writing letters to the stockholders, hundreds of them.

METCALFE

To the stockholders?

GILLIE

What's she doing that for?

SNELL

Some idea of Jack's—I don't know.

BLESSINGTON

Hold on! Just a moment! I didn't tell her to write to the stockholders. I said if any letters came in from the stockholders—

SNELL

Well, she's not waiting for 'em to come in.

GILLIE

What's *in* the letters—did you read 'em?

SNELL

Certainly I read 'em—some of them. Couldn't read 'em all.

GILLIE

What'd she say?

SNELL

Oh, how are you, and have they got any suggestions, and stuff like that.

METCALFE

Sounds harmless.

SNELL

What do *we* want with their suggestions? Damned fool idea in the first place, putting her in here. I must say, Jack, I didn't like the way you handled her, that day at the meeting.

BLESSINGTON

We've been over that a dozen times. She's here now, and we've got to keep her another three weeks. Do you want her to show up at the meeting again and raise hell!

SNELL

All I know is I don't like her writing those letters to the stockholders. It's not safe.

BLESSINGTON

What can we do about it? We can't fire her.

SNELL

I'll tell you what we can do about it. We can take her secretary away from her. Let her write six hundred letters a day by hand and see how she likes it.

(MISS L'ARRIERE *enters again. She is fully clothed, this time.*)

BLESSINGTON

Well? Something wrong, Miss L'Arriere?

MISS L'ARRIERE
(Indicating her hair)
"*I*'m wearing General Products bobby pins."

BLESSINGTON
(Looks her up and down. He doesn't like it)
That's no good—no good at all. Very disappointing, Miss L'Arriere. Tell Mr. Wilcox I don't like it at all.

MISS L'ARRIERE
Yes, Mr. Blessington.
(She goes.)

BLESSINGTON
(Outraged)
Sending a girl in here dressed like that! What the hell's he thinking of!
(And then the noon whistle blows.)

THE FOUR OF THEM
Lunch!
(They hurry out. Lunch is lunch.)

The Curtains Close

The Narrator

SO EVERY DAY CINDERELLA PUNCHED THE TIME CLOCK AND ATE WATER-CRESS SANDWICHES IN THE COMPANY CAFETERIA. NOW ONE DAY SHE WAS WORKING AWAY IN HER OFFICE, HER LITTLE HEAD FILLED WITH HAPPY THOUGHTS, AND WONDERING WHETHER PRINCE CHARMING AND THE GOLDEN COACH WERE EVER GOING TO COME ALONG. AND AS SHE BUBBLED AND TOILED, TRYING TO TURN AN HONEST BUCK, SHE DREAMED ABOUT THE TIME WHEN THE PRINCE WOULD FIT THE GLASS SLIPPER ONTO HER DAINTY FOOT. LITTLE DID SHE THINK, AS SHE SAT THERE, THAT WHAT SHE WAS GOING TO GET WAS NOT A GLASS SLIPPER, BUT A <u>GOOD SWIFT BOOT.</u>

Scene 4

LAURA PARTRIDGE's *office again.*
MRS. PARTRIDGE *is alone, and dictating into the machine in a brisk and businesslike manner.*

MRS. PARTRIDGE
(*Consulting a letter in her hand*)
. . . Salt Lake City, Utah. Dear Mrs. Avery, semicolon, paragraph. I was so delighted that you answered my letter of last week, period. Yes, comma, I have been in Salt Lake City twice, dash dash, once in 1906 and once in 1925, period. It is a beautiful city. I am so pleased that you are satisfied with the way General Products is being managed, period. I can assure you that earnings will be much higher for the next period, period. But remember, comma, dear Mrs. Avery, comma, if you ever have a suggestion to offer to your company, dash dash, I am always at the above address. I hope that I will hear from you again, comma, real soon, comma. I remain your new friend, and so forth, and so forth, et cetera.
(*She puts the letter on the desk; picks up another*)

Colonel William B. Butler, one-seven Ashton—A-s-h-t-o-n Street, Natchez, Miss. My dear Colonel, semi-colon, paragraph. Stop. Miss Shotgraven, use Form Letter for Men No. 5 here. And in the second paragraph insert, quote: "I have not had the pleasure of visiting your beautiful and romantic city since 1911, period. However, its memory is still with me, and I agree with you completely that Natchez is indeed the Jewel of the Swamps.

(*She stops as* MISS SHOTGRAVEN *enters, carrying a large stack of letters.* MISS SHOTGRAVEN *has been to that little hairdresser, and the severe hairdo has been exchanged for a curly sweep-up.*)

MISS SHOTGRAVEN

Form Letter for Women, No. 8. A thousand of them.

MRS. PARTRIDGE

Thank you, dear. It's nice to have them on hand.

MISS SHOTGRAVEN

Lucky I got there when I did. The mimeograph department was getting ready to close.

MRS. PARTRIDGE

This early?

MISS SHOTGRAVEN

It's a quarter to five, Mrs. Partridge.

MRS. PARTRIDGE

Oh, dear. Already? Time just seems to fly. . . . So much work. We *are* doing a good job, aren't we, Miss Shotgraven?

MISS SHOTGRAVEN

I think so.

MRS. PARTRIDGE

I think so, too.

(JENKINS, *from the mail room, comes in, a few letters in his hand.*)

JENKINS

Afternoon, Mrs. Partridge.

MRS. PARTRIDGE

Hello, Mark.

JENKINS

(*To* MISS SHOTGRAVEN)

Hi.

MISS SHOTGRAVEN

(*Primly*)

Good afternoon, Mr. Jenkins.

JENKINS

Few misdirected strays came in. Thought I'd deliver them myself.

(*Handing her the letters*)

MRS. PARTRIDGE

That's very kind of you, Mark.

JENKINS

Service—that's all.

(*To* MISS SHOTGRAVEN)

How about dinner tomorrow night?

MISS SHOTGRAVEN

All right.

JENKINS

And next week we gotta go to the Music Hall. They're putting in a new screen that's twice as wide as the theatre.

(*He goes.*)

MRS. PARTRIDGE

Well! Next time I'm up around 53rd Street, I'm certainly going to drop in and compliment that little hairdresser.

MISS SHOTGRAVEN
(*Changing the subject*)
I—I passed Mr. Snell's secretary in the hall. She gave me a memo for you.

MRS. PARTRIDGE

Thank you, dear.
(*She glances at the memo and is rocked by what she reads*)
Oh!

MISS SHOTGRAVEN

Mrs. Partridge!

MRS. PARTRIDGE

They're—taking you away from me, Miss Shotgraven.

MISS SHOTGRAVEN

What?

Mr. Snell. He says there's a retrenchment policy. And you have to leave. As of the close of this business day. That means—now.

MISS SHOTGRAVEN

But I don't want to leave you, Mrs. Partridge.

MRS. PARTRIDGE

What'll I do? I don't know how to typewrite. I don't know where the mimeograph department is. Or where they keep the postage stamps.

MISS SHOTGRAVEN

Perhaps I could drop in during my lunch hour, Mrs. Partridge.

MRS. PARTRIDGE

You are a very lovable young lady, Miss Shotgraven. And staunch, too. But, no. All of this will have to stop now.

MISS SHOTGRAVEN

I—I don't know what to say.

MRS. PARTRIDGE

They don't want me here. They don't want me here at all.

MISS SHOTGRAVEN

Mrs. Partridge, I'd like you to know that every minute I've worked for you . . .

(*She chokes up; goes for her hat and purse.*)

MRS. PARTRIDGE

Miss Shotgraven, before you go, would you type one little note for me? Just make it a memo. *From:* Laura Partridge, *to:* Mr. Clifford Snell. Until now, I have enjoyed working for the General Products Corporation. As my usefulness is at an end, please accept my resignation. . . . Will you typewrite that now, dear?

MISS SHOTGRAVEN

No. Mrs. Partridge, this is a large organization. Sit here. Collect your check every week.

MRS. PARTRIDGE

It's getting late, dear. . . . Would you mind?

MISS SHOTGRAVEN

Do you want me to drop it at Mr. Snell's office on the way out?

MRS. PARTRIDGE

Would you?

MISS SHOTGRAVEN

Mrs. Partridge . . .

MRS. PARTRIDGE

What is it, dear?
(*Her eyes, unseeing, are on another letter.*)

MISS SHOTGRAVEN

Good-bye.

MRS. PARTRIDGE

Thank you for everything, Amelia.
(MISS SHOTGRAVEN *goes.* MRS. PARTRIDGE *concentrates a little more on the letter before her, as though to check her own emotion. Presently she is actually reading it. She concentrates a little more —now she is both reading it and digesting it. She jumps to her feet*)
Miss Shotgraven! . . . Miss Shotgraven!
(MISS SHOTGRAVEN *returns, hurriedly.*)

MISS SHOTGRAVEN

Yes, Mrs. Partridge?

MRS. PARTRIDGE

Miss Shotgraven, did you read the Company newspaper this morning? Didn't it say that General Products had eliminated one of its competitors—some company that makes clocks or something up in Pittsfield?

MISS SHOTGRAVEN

I—believe so. But—

MRS. PARTRIDGE

Then listen to this. It's from Pittsfield. "I received your letter and am writing to you right away because the strangest thing has happened. My husband has just lost his job after working for the same company for twenty-two years. It is one of our best companies here—the Apex Electric Clock Company. And the funny thing is that General Products bought the company just two years ago, and now everybody is saying that it was General Products that drove it out of business. Why would they do that to their own company, is what I want to know. Please answer as soon as possible."

MISS SHOTGRAVEN

I don't understand.

MRS. PARTRIDGE

Neither do I. . . . I wonder if it's true.
  (*Takes up the phone*)
Long distance!
  (*Back to* MISS SHOTGRAVEN)
It does seem a funny thing to do, doesn't it—put one of their own companies out of business!
  (*Back to the phone*)
I want Pittsfield, Massachusetts. I want the telephone number of Mrs. Henry Brooks, 141 Oak Street. . . . I'll pay for the call myself—this is Mrs. Partridge speaking.

MISS SHOTGRAVEN

Don't bother checking, Mrs. Partridge! It's our own company, all right. Here it is in our directory.

(*Reads*)

"Clocks, pendulum—General Products Divisions: Moline, Illinois, Baton Rouge, Louisiana; San Bernardino, California. . . . Clocks, electric: Apex Electric Clock Company, Pittsfield, Massachusetts!

MRS. PARTRIDGE

Cancel the call, operator!
(*She hangs up.*)

MISS SHOTGRAVEN

What do you make of it?

MRS. PARTRIDGE

Their own company! Putting it into bankruptcy and it's their own company! . . . Boy! What I can do with this at the next stockholders' meeting!
(*The phone again*)
Mr. Snell's office, please! . . . What did you do with my resignation?

MISS SHOTGRAVEN

I put it in Mr. Snell's box.

MRS. PARTRIDGE

Get it back!

MISS SHOTGRAVEN

I can't! It's locked!

MRS. PARTRIDGE

Break it open!
(*Into telephone*)
I want to talk to Mr. Snell! . . . Take an axe if you

want to—I guarantee he won't say a word! Those big geniuses! . . . Gone for the day! Well, it's pretty early for *him* to be waltzing out. . . . Yes, you *can* give him a message. What does he mean by taking away my secretary! . . . This is Laura Partridge! . . . Yes, that's what I said, and tell him I'll be in to see him first thing in the morning. And I want those three other dummies there too. Good-bye!

(*She hangs up with a bang.*)

The Curtains Close

The Narrator

SO THE FOUR UGLY CORPORATION DIRECTORS TORE THEIR HAIR AND GNASHED THEIR TEETH, WHICH DID NOT MAKE THEM ANY LESS UGLY, AS YOU CAN IMAGINE. BUT NO MATTER HOW MUCH THEY SQUIRMED, ONE SIMPLE LITTLE FACT REMAINED: CINDERELLA HAD THEM BY THE <u>SWANNEE RIVER</u>.

Scene 5

The big office again.
The Board of Directors are seated in discomfort on the edges of their chairs, like schoolboys. Behind the desk sits MRS. PARTRIDGE, *enjoying herself in the big chair.*

MRS. PARTRIDGE

Now let's see. Miss Shotgraven comes back to work as my secretary.
(*She makes a big check mark on a list before her*)
Agreed?

BLESSINGTON

(*Swallowing hard*)
Agreed.

MRS. PARTRIDGE

And she gets a ten dollar a week raise?
(*Another check mark*)
Is that agreed, Mr. Snell?

SNELL

(*Nearly choking on the words*)
That's—right.

MRS. PARTRIDGE

And I can mail all the letters I want to? . . . That's agreed, too?
(*They nod glumly*)
Now, what else was there?

BLESSINGTON

(*After a pause*)
Do you—do you mind if I smoke, Mrs. Partridge?

MRS. PARTRIDGE

Oh, good heavens no, go right ahead. It's your office, all
of you. I do hope you're comfortable—those little chairs.

BLESSINGTON

Yes, indeed. Are you comfortable in that chair, Mrs.
Partridge?

MRS. PARTRIDGE

(*Leaning back luxuriously*)
Oh, very comfortable, thank you.
(*The phone rings.*)

GILLIE

McKeever!

METCALFE

This must be our call. Do you mind, Mrs. Partridge?

MRS. PARTRIDGE

(*Rises*)
Not at all.

METCALFE

(*Taking the phone*)
Yeah? . . . I'm ready.
(*Covering mouthpiece*)
Washington . . . It's McKeever, all right.

BLESSINGTON

Be nice to him.

63

SNELL

Nice nothing! Give him the facts.

METCALFE

Hello, Ed. . . . Gosh, it's good to hear your voice again. How are you? . . . That's great. . . . Oh, just sitting around your old office. Cliff, and Jack, and Warren, and —uh—
(*He decides not to mention* MRS. PARTRIDGE, *natch*)
. . . No, I finished the lamp table. Working on a chair now. Early American.

BLESSINGTON

Let *me* talk to him. . . . How've you been, Ed? . . . That's splendid . . . How'd you like yourself on the cover of *Time* last week? Looked very impressive, I thought. . . .

SNELL

Oh, for God's—give it to me! . . . McKeever, this is Cliff Snell. . . . Look, we can't understand why we haven't been awarded any Government contracts this year. . . . I'm aware there's no law that we have to get 'em. . . . Well, don't you think that if you looked into it personally . . . I'm aware it's up to the Government, but if you were to . . . Hello . . . Hello.
(*Realizes he has hung up*)
Won't even talk about it.

BLESSINGTON

There's gratitude for you. After that half-million dollar bonus we gave him.

SNELL

He didn't take it.

BLESSINGTON

He didn't? Where is it?

SNELL

It's in the treasury.

BLESSINGTON

What treasury?

SNELL

Ours, of course. Whose did you think?

BLESSINGTON

I was afraid you meant the United States Treasury.

SNELL

I can understand his being careful, but not to award us a single contract! Just because he used to head the company!

MRS. PARTRIDGE

But I don't think that's fair.

BLESSINGTON

Of *course* it isn't fair!

MRS. PARTRIDGE

What do I write my stockholders about the dividend?

SNELL

(*Annoyed*)

Write 'em that because there's a stubborn old goat in Washington, the dividend will be less, that's all.

MRS. PARTRIDGE

But I've already written them that the dividend will be higher this year. They'll be so disappointed.

SNELL

Tell 'em to blame Ed McKeever, not us.

MRS. PARTRIDGE

I just can't do it. Those poor stockholders—the little ones, I mean.

GILLIE

The little ones don't lose as much as the big ones.

SNELL

We're sorry about the little stockholders, Mrs. Partridge, but they've got to take it as it comes. And it's not coming.

MRS. PARTRIDGE

But suppose I talked to Mr. McKeever, and told him about the little stockholders? You see, I've *promised* them.

GILLIE

I'm afraid it wouldn't do any good, Mrs. Partridge.

BLESSINGTON

No.

METCALFE

(*Slowly*)
Mrs. Partridge is mighty good at talking.

BLESSINGTON

(*Thinks it out*)

And she does represent the little stockholders. She's one herself.

GILLIE

He just might listen to her.

SNELL

(*A quick decision*)

Get him back on the phone!

METCALFE

That's no good. She's got to talk to him—face to face.

BLESSINGTON

Exactly the way she's just done with us.

SNELL

(*Wheeling on* MRS. PARTRIDGE)

Do you think you could do it? . . . Would you, Mrs. Partridge, go down to Washington, and tell Mr. McKeever about the little stockholders?

GILLIE

Just the little ones, mind you!

BLESSINGTON

Don't mention the big ones!

MRS. PARTRIDGE

Well, if you think I could do any good . . .

BLESSINGTON

Certainly you could do good. Take some of their letters along.

MRS. PARTRIDGE

Yes . . . Yes . . . When would you want me to go?

METCALFE

The sooner the better!

BLESSINGTON

Tomorrow! Can you go tomorrow?

MRS. PARTRIDGE

I—I guess so. What time?

BLESSINGTON

Eight-thirty train! Would you mind, *one morning,* eight-thirty?

SNELL

Just one morning.

MRS. PARTRIDGE

But—what do I do?

SNELL

Just tell him about the little stockholders!

GILLIE

The littler the better!

MRS. PARTRIDGE

Yes, I know, but—

BLESSINGTON

We'll get you a ticket—drawing room, everything!

MRS. PARTRIDGE

But—when I get to Washington—

BLESSINGTON

We'll have somebody at the station—take you right to him. All you've got to do is to talk!

METCALFE

Just the way you did here.

GILLIE

Remember the little stockholders!

MRS. PARTRIDGE

(*The big decision*)

I'll do it!

SNELL

Good for you!

METCALFE

That's great!

BLESSINGTON

Good luck!

GILLIE

And thank you, Mrs. Partridge.

MRS. PARTRIDGE

You're welcome.

BLESSINGTON

I can't tell you how grateful we all are.

MRS. PARTRIDGE

Oh, that's all right—well—I won't see you gentlemen again, then, before I . . . Good-bye. . . . Good-bye. . . . Good-bye. . . . Good-bye.
(*She makes the rounds*)
I'll just tell him it isn't fair.

GILLIE

To the little stockholders!

SNELL

And make him listen to you!

MRS. PARTRIDGE

Now don't you worry about a thing. Any of you.
(*She addresses them all*)
I've played Washington before.
(*She goes.*)

The Curtains Close

The Narrator

SO CINDERELLA WENT TO MEET HER PRINCE CHARMING. PRINCE CHARMING WAS BALD AS A HONEYDEW AND FIFTEEN POUNDS OVERWEIGHT, BUT HE ALSO HAD FIFTEEN MILLION DOLLARS, WHICH DID NOT MAKE HIM ANY LESS CHARMING, AS YOU CAN IMAGINE. RIGHT NOW THE PRINCE HAD THE ENTIRE UNITED STATES GOVERNMENT ON HIS NECK, AND IT IS WELL KNOWN THAT THE PENTAGON ALONE WEIGHS FOUR HUNDRED MILLION TONS.

Scene 6

MC KEEVER'S *office in Washington.*
*An enormous room with an enormous desk—on
it a phone and nothing else. In the background an
American flag.*
MC KEEVER *is alone in the room. In his shirt
sleeves, he is pacing and reading a report.
The phone rings. It will ring a lot.*

MC KEEVER

McKeever! . . . Clarence! . . . What the hell happened
to South America? . . . I know it's down there, but
what's happening? . . . And where are those cruisers?
. . . What cruisers do you think? The same ones that I've
been yelling about for six months! . . . Well, I want a
meeting of all bureau chiefs tomorrow morning at eight
o'clock. Fly 'em in—I want 'em here.
(*Puts down the report. Takes off coat; runs around
the desk*)

(MISS LOGAN, *his secretary, enters with a letter for
him to sign. The phone rings*)

McKeever! . . . The note to Malenkov? How do *I*
know? . . . Just Moscow, Russia, ought to reach him.
(*Hangs up. Growls to himself*)
Call me for everything!
(*He starts a squatting exercise.* MISS LOGAN *enters*

72

*with a newspaper. He continues squatting up and
down. She starts to squat up and down in unison
with him as he reads the paper*) (*The phone rings*)
McKeever! . . . No, I can't give you the dato on Nato—
the Nato on data—

(*Desperate, but gets it out*)

The data on Nato!

(*He stretches out on the desk and starts doing a
bicycle exercise.*)

(*The phone rings again*)

Miss Logan!

(MISS LOGAN *runs on, picks up the phone and puts
it to his ear*)

McKeever! . . . No! We can't christen any more ships
with champagne. Use seltzer. We're trying to balance the
budget.

(*He flops back on the desk again.*)

(MISS LOGAN *replaces the phone, then kneels down
beside him and whispers in his ear*)

Who?

(*She whispers again*)

Send her in.

(*He gets off his desk and dons his coat*)

(*Meanwhile* MISS LOGAN *ushers in* MRS. PARTRIDGE.
*She has donned her best bib and tucker for the
occasion.*)

MRS. PARTRIDGE

How do you do?

MC KEEVER

How do you do? Now I'll do all the talking! I've got to make this fast, because any minute the phone'll ring and it'll be the goddam Senate wanting me to come over for some more questions. The Senate, Mrs.—you're Mrs.—uh—

MRS. PARTRIDGE

Partridge. Mr. Blessington said—

MC KEEVER

Yes. Jack Blessington told me you were coming. The Senate, Mrs. Partridge, is driving me crazy. Absolutely crazy! I'm there every day, seems to me. Just settling down to work here, getting out the stuff, and bang! The goddam Senate says come over and answer questions—what I'm doing, what I'm not doing, *why*! A Senator, Mrs. Partridge, is the only man on God's green earth who is allowed to talk forever without knowing what he's talking about and nobody can stop him! Nobody! Greatest time-waster in the world, the United States Senate, and there's nothing anybody can do about it! Absolutely nothing! I'm there for hours—days! Weeks!

MRS. PARTRIDGE

Well—

MC KEEVER

(*As the phone rings*)
McKeever! . . . NO! The French can't have it!
(*Hangs up*)
Now, I know why you're here, Mrs. Partridge—I know just what you're after! The answer is NO.

74

MRS. PARTRIDGE

But—

MC KEEVER

Remember—this isn't business, down here. Not like business at all. I've made a discovery, here in Washington, and I'll tell you what it is. Honesty! Just plain honesty. I'm not used to it yet, but I'm starting to get the hang of it. Been in business all my life and a man can't change overnight. Anyhow, I'm working on it, and in another month or so I'll turn the trick. Because if you're not honest down here they catch you at it and then you *do* get hell.

(*The phone rings*)

McKeever! . . . Okay for the Eskimos.

(*Hangs up*)

So the answer is no. No contracts for General Products, Mrs. Partridge!

(*He is now reading and signing still another report*)

Because if I give 'em to 'em the goddam Senate will be on my neck and I've had about all I can stand.

MRS. PARTRIDGE

You know, I sort of thought you'd be a big silent man. You're big, but you're not silent.

MC KEEVER

I've got nothing to be silent about.

MRS. PARTRIDGE

Now, why don't you sit down behind that desk and just be silent! It'll be good for you. Go on. Try it.

(MC KEEVER *looks at her a second, then, as though hypnotized, sits in his chair. He looks at her for the next move.*)

MRS. PARTRIDGE

Fine! . . . I'd have known you anywhere. You look just like your bust downstairs.

MC KEEVER

That isn't me. That's Stonewall Jackson.

MRS. PARTRIDGE

Oh, not here. Downstairs in the General Products Building.

MC KEEVER

Oh!
        (*He gets interested*)
There's a bust of me in the General Products Building?

MRS. PARTRIDGE

Yes, didn't you know? . . . It's very good, too.

MC KEEVER

A statue, eh? . . . Now, they didn't have to go and do a thing like that. How big is it?

MRS. PARTRIDGE

Oh, it's big.
        (*She indicates the size.*)

MC KEEVER

Whereabouts is it?

MRS. PARTRIDGE

Right across from the elevators. So it's the first thing you see coming in and going out.

MC KEEVER

Yeah?

MRS. PARTRIDGE

And on dark days there's a light in the ceiling that shines right down on your head.

MC KEEVER

Sort of a halo.

MRS. PARTRIDGE

Now don't tell me they forgot to write you about it.

MC KEEVER

I don't see a third of the mail that comes in. No time. And if I do get a minute the goddam Senate—

MRS. PARTRIDGE

Now, now!

MC KEEVER

What's the matter?

MRS. PARTRIDGE

You mustn't even think about the goddam Senate. That's what gets you all worked up.

MC KEEVER

How can I keep from thinking about it when—

MRS. PARTRIDGE

It just occurred to me. Are you Taurus the Bull?

MC KEEVER

How's that?

MRS. PARTRIDGE

I'm Leo the Lion. I was born July 25th. When's your birthday?

MC KEEVER

April 7th.

MRS. PARTRIDGE

Oh! You're Aries the Ram. No wonder you're successful in business. J. P. Morgan was a Ram too.

MC KEEVER

I don't think I'm following you, Mrs. Partridge.

MRS. PARTRIDGE

I have a hobby. Horoscopes.

MC KEEVER

Horoscopes? . . . Really? Can you tell fortunes?

MRS. PARTRIDGE

Heavens, no. That sort of thing is silly. But the Zodiac— it may not always be accurate, but you'd be surprised how often—well, let's take *you,* for example. You're a regular Ram. I can understand how you did all those things with General Products. Building it up to such a big company.

MC KEEVER

Tell me, Mrs. Partridge, how long have you been with the company?

MRS. PARTRIDGE

Not long.

MC KEEVER

What company you with before that?

MRS. PARTRIDGE

I wasn't with a company before. I was on the stage.

MC KEEVER

(*High interest*)
The stage? You mean an actress?

MRS. PARTRIDGE

Forty-six productions.

MC KEEVER

You don't say? You know something? I always had an idea *I*'d have liked to've been an actor.

MRS. PARTRIDGE

Oh, I'm glad you didn't, Mr. McKeever. It's a terrible business.

MC KEEVER

Always kind of fascinated me. Clyde Fitch, Shakespeare —did you ever do Shakespeare, Mrs. Partridge?

MRS. PARTRIDGE

Little bit. Not much.

MC KEEVER

Must have been wonderful.

MRS. PARTRIDGE

I never cared much for Shakespeare. He's so tiring. You never get to sit down unless you're a king.

MC KEEVER

I used to recite a lot when I was a boy. All kinds of things. Then—I didn't know—something happened—all of a sudden I was a businessman.

MRS. PARTRIDGE

You're lucky. Almost nobody makes a living in the theatre any more.

MC KEEVER

People used to think I was pretty good—well, for an amateur. Used to do recitations Friday afternoons—you know, in school.

MRS. PARTRIDGE

Oh, I'm glad you didn't go on the stage, Mr. McKeever. You're better off even *here.*

MC KEEVER

Still, would have been fun. Had one recitation—they used to applaud like anything after I finished.

MRS. PARTRIDGE

The applause is very nice, but the rest of it!

MC KEEVER

Then Professor Sleeth—that was our elocution teacher—he had me do it for the parents and everybody at the end of the term. They put it in the paper—nice write-up. "Spoke with real fire," it said. "Real fire."

MRS. PARTRIDGE

That's a good notice.

MC KEEVER

"Spartacus to the Gladiators."

MRS. PARTRIDGE

What?

MC KEEVER

That was the name of the piece—"Spartacus to the Gladiators."

MRS. PARTRIDGE

Oh.

MC KEEVER

You know, I still remember it.

MRS. PARTRIDGE

Really? Well, that happens—something that you learned when you were young, why, all your life—

MC KEEVER

"Ye call me Chief"—you wouldn't do me a big favor and listen to it, would you?—tell me what you really think?

MRS. PARTRIDGE

I'd love to.

MC KEEVER

Mind you, if you don't like it, say so.

MRS. PARTRIDGE

Oh, I will. Whenever I go backstage to somebody's dressing room . . .

MC KEEVER

Because *hell*! I'm never going to be an actor *now*! Be foolish, at my age.

(*Hopefully*)
Wouldn't it?

MRS. PARTRIDGE

Yes, it would.

MC KEEVER

(*Not the answer he wanted*)
Uh—yes . . . Anyhow, here it is. I haven't done this for
years, mind you.

MRS. PARTRIDGE

I know.

MC KEEVER

Not since I was a boy.
(*All over again*)
"Spartacus to the Gladiators":

(NOTE: *This recitation is accompanied by overdra-
matic gestures. You'll just have to imagine them*)

"Ye call me chief, and ye do well to call me chief who, for
twelve long years, has met in the arena every shape of
man and beast that the broad empire of Rome could fur-
nish and has never yet lowered his arm. And yet I was not
always thus, the savage chief of still more savage men.
My ancestors came from old Sparta and settled among the
vine-clad hills and citron groves of Cyracella. My early
life ran quiet as the brook by which I sported. And when,
at noon, I gathered the sheep beneath the shade and
played upon my shepherd's flute, there was a friend, the
son of a neighbor, who joined me in my pastime. One
evening after the sheep were folded and we were seated
beneath the myrtle which girded our cottage, my grand-

sire—an old man—was telling of Marathon and how a little band of Spartans, in a defile of the mountain, had withstood a whole army. I knew not then what war was, but my cheeks burned—I knew not why—and I grasped the knees of that venerable man until my mother, parting the hair from off my forehead, kissed my throbbing temples and bade me go to rest and think no more of savage wars. . . . That night the Romans landed on our coast. I saw the bleeding body of my father cast among the blazing rafters of our dwelling. . . . Today I killed a man in the arena. And when I broke his helmet clasp, behold! he was my boyhood friend. He knew me, smiled faintly, gasped, and died. The same sweet smile that I had marked when, in adventurous boyhood, we had scaled the lofty cliff to pluck the first ripe grape and bear it home in childish triumph. I told the Praetor that the dead man had been my friend and begged that I might bear away the body to burn it on the funeral pyre and mourn over it in silence. Aye, amid the dust of the arena did I beg that poor boon. But the Praetor drew back as though I were pollution and sternly said, "Let the carrion rot. There are no noblemen but Romans."

(*He bows to* MRS. PARTRIDGE *by way of signifying its finish. And about time.*)

MRS. PARTRIDGE

Oh, I'm awfully glad you didn't try to be an actor, Mr. McKeever.

MC KEEVER

You are?

MRS. PARTRIDGE

Yes, because—

83

MC KEEVER

(*The phone rings*)

McKeever! . . . Oh, good morning, Senator! . . . Yes, I'm fine. And you? . . . Did you read my report? . . . Well, just between us, what did you think of it? . . . What? . . . Before your committee? . . . But I was there yesterday. And twice last week.

(*Sighs heavily*)

Very well, Senator. . . . Nine-thirty tomorrow morning. . . . Copies of all contracts. I'll be there.

(*Hangs up*)

Well, there you are! . . . How they expect a man to get anything done—Miss Logan!—When he has to keep running to those committee rooms all the time—Miss Logan!

(*She enters*)

Get everything ready—every contract, every letter! Every memorandum! I'm up before the goddam Senate again tomorrow morning.

(*Pacing*)

Enough to drive a man crazy! Senate, Senate, Senate!

MRS. PARTRIDGE

Poor Mr. McKeever! Why do you do it?

MC KEEVER

What?

MRS. PARTRIDGE

Why don't you refuse?

MC KEEVER

Refuse! It's the goddam Senate!

MRS. PARTRIDGE

Then why don't you quit?

MC KEEVER

What do you mean—quit?

MRS. PARTRIDGE

Just quit! Walk out and don't come back. You don't *have* to do this, Mr. McKeever—not if it's going to do this to you.

MC KEEVER

That's so, I don't.

MRS. PARTRIDGE

Besides, they need you back at General Products. I didn't want to come right out and say so, but those other men are terrible. They're going to ruin the company. There won't be any dividends at all.

MC KEEVER

Ruin the company? Miss Logan! . . . Mrs. Partridge, would you have lunch with me and talk some more about this?

MRS. PARTRIDGE

I'd be glad to.

MC KEEVER

I'm going out to lunch, Miss Logan. I'll be back in an hour—*two* hours, I don't know. . . . Where would you like to eat, Mrs. Partridge? Anywhere you say.

MRS. PARTRIDGE

You know what I've heard a lot about—where I'd love
to go? The Senate Restaurant.

MC KEEVER

Oh, my God!

The Curtains Close

Scene 7

A giant television set.
A few wavy lines on the screen and an image comes into focus.

Sound: A bell

A VOICE

The Six o'clock News Round-up, Bill Parker Reporting!

(*We see a newsroom, teletype machines clanging, clocks in background. A chair, microphone, a reporter*)

PARKER

Good evening, ladies and gentlemen—here are the headlines. A resignation in Washington, a tornado in Texas, and a lady with fourteen children in Alaska sells her cow! Now let's have a look at the top story of the day. This afternoon, in the nation's capital, one of the Government's key figures, Edward L. McKeever, handed in his resignation. Members of both parties were stunned. Senate leaders in particular are at a loss as to why McKeever decided to leave Washington. And here are first films rushed directly to our newsroom of McKeever as he left the nation's capital this afternoon.

(The film shows MC KEEVER *standing beside a plane. In front of him is a reporter with cable and microphone.)*

REPORTER

What significance, Mr. McKeever, does your resignation have?

MC KEEVER

I just decided to quit. No significance. No significance at all.

(Back to the Announcer)

PARKER

Mr. McKeever was accompanied by an unidentified friend.

(Shot of LAURA PARTRIDGE *as* MC KEEVER *helps her up the first step. She turns, apparently in response to a question. There is an enigmatic smile on her face.)*
(More wavy lines on the screen, indicating a passage of time)
(Another newsroom. A map on the wall, a new reporter sitting behind another desk)

REPORTER

A very good evening, ladies and gentlemen. This is Dwight Brookfield bringing the eleven o'clock news right into your own living room. And the big news tonight still centers about the sudden move made earlier today—

a move *out* of Washington, *out* of the Government. One high administration source was quoted as saying that McKeever's abrupt departure is causing grave inconvenience to certain parties in certain parties. McKeever, meanwhile, was undergoing an inconvenience of his own. Heavy thunderstorms over the Middle Atlantic States forced his plane down in Philadelphia a few hours ago. Told of the furore his action had caused in Washington, Mr. McKeever refused to comment.

(MC KEEVER *and* LAURA PARTRIDGE *are seen descending the plane stairway, greeted by reporters.*)

MC KEEVER

Sorry, boys, no comment. I'm not a talker, you know.

(*Back to the studio*)

REPORTER

Mr. McKeever was accompanied by a woman reported to be a business associate.

(MC KEEVER *steps aside—and guess who has been behind him all the time. You're right*)
(*More wavy lines and again a passage of time*)
(*This time it is a woman reporter—behind her a bookcase flanked by two windows with chintzy curtains.*)

A VOICE

And now, Estelle Evans and the high noon news bulletins, a compendium of events of local, national and international importance to you and your family. . . . Miss Evans.

MISS EVANS

Good afternoon, ladies. I'll have the weather, the fashions and the shopping for you in just a second. But first, I'd like to tell you in word *and* picture about the latest developments in a front-page story that I know will interest you as much as it fascinates me. Edward L. McKeever— you all know who *he* is—he resigned from that big job in Washington yesterday—well, this morning Mr. McKeever arrived at his New York office from Philadelphia. *And* —this is what will interest you ladies—still accompanying him was the mystery woman who traveled with him from Washington late last night.

(*Shot of* MC KEEVER *and* LAURA *getting out of a limousine in front of the General Products building*)

A REPORTER

Pardon me, lady, would you mind telling us who you are?

MRS. PARTRIDGE

Oh, I'm not anybody. Not anybody at all.

(*Back to the studio*)

MISS EVANS

Well! Despite the mystery woman's denial, informed circles in Washington were busy speculating this morning on the strange circumstances of Mr. McKeever's resignation. Did he break with the administration or did the millionaire widower leave his high post because of a woman? In other words, ladies, is Edward McKeever a modern Marc Anthony, captivated by a wily and seductive Cleopatra?

(The television set goes off.)

Scene 8

Back at General Products.
MC KEEVER *is at the desk—the other directors grouped at his side.*
Several reporters are present, and they have apparently been giving MC KEEVER *a time.*
The flashlights snap.

MC KEEVER

All right, boys, that's enough pictures! Let's run this just the way the President runs his conferences. First a statement, then questions.

A. P. MAN

Excuse me, Mr. McKeever—Sullivan, A. P.

MC KEEVER

Questions afterwards—here's your statement. Ready?

U. P. MAN

I'm Turner, Mr. McKeever—U. P.

I. N. S.

Mathewson, I. N. S. We'd like—

MC KEEVER

I know what you'd like—get out your pencils. I'm only going to say it once, so get it down. "Political differences had absolutely no bearing on my resignation. My confidence in the Administration and its policies—"

I. N. S.

Sorry, Mr. McKeever—that's not the story we're after.

U. P.

What about the woman?

A. P.

Yeah—who's the woman?

MC KEEVER

Nobody at all.

BLESSINGTON

Nobody at all.
  (*The three other men murmur assent.*)

MC KEEVER

Just an old friend.

I. N. S.

Where is she?

A. P.

What's her name?

MC KEEVER

Her name is Mrs. Laura Partridge and she works for this company.

BLESSINGTON

Yes.

MC KEEVER

She came to see me on business and *that's all.*

BLESSINGTON

Absolutely all.

(*The other men agree. They will agree to* any*thing, in their present spot.*)

U. P.

Where is she?

I. N. S.

Can we see her?

MC KEEVER

Certainly. We have nothing to conceal. Always willing to co-operate with the press.

BLESSINGTON

Yes indeed.

MC KEEVER

Come in, Mrs. Partridge.
(MRS. PARTRIDGE *enters—somewhat cautiously. It is clear that this entrance has been rehearsed.*)

U. P.

How do you do, Mrs. Partridge?

MRS. PARTRIDGE

(*Carefully*)
How do you do?

94

U. P.

You work for the company, Mrs. Partridge?

MC KEEVER

Yes, she does.
(*The other men concur.*)

MRS. PARTRIDGE

Yes, I do.

I. N. S.

Doing what?

MC KEEVER

She's in charge of—er—

BLESSINGTON

Of stockholder relations.

MRS. PARTRIDGE

I'm in charge of stockholder relations.

MC KEEVER

(*Somewhat gratuitous*)
She's in charge of stockholder relations.

A. P.

Why did you go to see Mr. McKeever?

MC KEEVER

She came to see me on business.

BLESSINGTON

Yes. On business.
> (*The others agree.*)

MRS. PARTRIDGE

I went to see him on business.

U. P.

Had you known him long?

MC KEEVER

No, no.
> (*The other men deny it also.*)

MRS. PARTRIDGE

Goodness, no. I hadn't met him until yesterday.

I. N. S.

You left Washington yesterday afternoon.

MC KEEVER

Yes, she did.
> (*More concurring*)

MRS. PARTRIDGE

Yes, I did.

U. P.

And you got here this morning?

MC KEEVER

Yes, sir.
> (*The yes-men are right on the job.*)

MRS. PARTRIDGE

Yes, sir.

I. N. S.

Where did you spend the night?

MC KEEVER
(*He had not expected this*)

Why—uh—

THE OTHER MEN

Uh—
(*But they are stumped*)

MRS. PARTRIDGE
(*This one had not been rehearsed, but she is an honest woman*)

We were at the Hotel Barclay in Philadelphia.

MC KEEVER
(*Quickly*)

On separate floors!

THE FOUR OTHER MEN

Separate floors!

MRS. PARTRIDGE
(*A little late, would you say?*)

On separate floors.

(*But the newspaper boys have swung into action. A couple of them whip* MRS. PARTRIDGE *up onto the*

97

desk. One and all are ready with their cameras)
(MC KEEVER and the four stooges don't even want
to look. They turn away, hiding their faces fran-
tically beneath their coattails.)

MRS. PARTRIDGE
(Smoothing down her ruffled skirt)
Now, now! No cheesecake!

(The flashlights pop. And it is rather surprising, in
the circumstances, that a couple of arteries don't
pop too.)

The Curtain Falls on Act One

ACT TWO

As the act opens, the following curtain is revealed:

Scene 1

The General Products office again.

The office is empty. But just when you are beginning to think that the boys have all shot themselves, BLESSINGTON *enters—a pile of newspapers under his arm.*

He settles down at the desk; reads busily if not happily.

METCALFE *is next. Also with papers.*

METCALFE

Have you seen the papers?
(*Getting no answer, he too settles down to read*)
(*Then* WARREN GILLIE. *More papers*)

GILLIE

(*He has the hard luck to pick the same line*)
Have you seen the papers?

BLESSINGTON

(*With full sarcasm*)
No, Warren, we have *not seen* the *papers*. For the past twenty-four hours we have been living in a tree.

GILLIE

Well, what are we going to do about it? It's dreadful.

BLESSINGTON

It's not as bad for you as it is for me. You're not married.

GILLIE

I don't see what that's got to do with it.

BLESSINGTON

Well, if you were married to Mrs. Blessington you'd damn well see! According to her, *I* took that woman to Philadelphia.

GILLIE

Well, at choir practice last night, the whole choir was buzzing about it. Right in the middle of a Handel oratorio.

METCALFE

What's there to buzz about? This has got nothing to do with General Products!

BLESSINGTON

She works for us, doesn't she? The Partridge woman!

METCALFE

A lot of women work for us. Maybe they've *all* been to Philadelphia.

BLESSINGTON

Just the same, it's not good for the company. We sell things for the *home,* don't forget. Have you seen the wires we got this morning? Have you heard about the phone calls?

GILLIE

I've got an idea. Why don't we take a big ad? Full page in every paper in the country.

METCALFE

What'll we say in it?

GILLIE

Well, I . . . haven't gotten that far yet.

METCALFE

"Take a General Products diesel locomotive next time you go to Philadelphia."

GILLIE

Well, it wouldn't cost anything. It would come off taxes. And, maybe we could get that Hotel Barclay in Philadelphia to pay part of it.

BLESSINGTON

We've got to get rid of her, that's all.

METCALFE

We can't do that. That would only make it look worse.

BLESSINGTON

Well, if we don't get rid of her, it looks as though we're afraid of her.

GILLIE

Well, aren't we?
    (CLIFFORD SNELL *arrives.*)

SNELL

Well, I hope you're satisfied! You boys have got us in a hell of a spot.

BLESSINGTON

This wasn't any idea of mine, Clifford. When I go to Philadelphia, I always stay at the Bellevue-Stratford.

SNELL

I don't give a damn about Philadelphia. It's her bringing McKeever back that's going to make trouble.

BLESSINGTON

You don't think he's going to want his old job again, do you?

SNELL

I know this. He's going through the building right now shaking hands with all the employees.

GILLIE

What's he doing that for?

SNELL

How do I know? Some habit he picked up in Washington.

BLESSINGTON

But if he comes back he'll want to be Chairman of the Board again.

METCALFE

And President of the company.

BLESSINGTON

A lousy Vice-President again. Back to the masses.

SNELL

Now, listen. . . . If the four of us stick together, we can freeze him out. We've got the votes, haven't we?

BLESSINGTON

True enough.

GILLIE

Do you think we should?

METCALFE

I don't like doing this to Ed.

SNELL

We've got to do it. You want to keep your jobs, don't you? Your bonuses? Your stock options?

GILLIE

(*A thoughtful pause*)
Well—if you put it *that* way.

SNELL

Then don't any of you weaken. McKeever's a hell of a talker.

BLESSINGTON

But what about the woman? God knows what she's going to do next!

SNELL

Leave the woman to me.

METCALFE

Think you know how to handle her, Cliff?

SNELL

I know how to keep her away from the stockholders' meeting. And that's the main thing!

BLESSINGTON

How?

GILLIE

Yes, how?

SNELL

While you boys have been reading those newspapers, *I've* been doing some thinking. There's one sure way to reach her. Astrology.
> (*He unrolls a horoscope chart which he brought in with him*)

Now, here's the way this thing works.
> (*He looks them over*)

Once you're born, you're done for.
> (*The heads of the four uglies come closer together as they study the chart.*)
> (*The lights fade.*)

The Narrator

WELL, I WOULDN'T SAY THAT THE BOYS WERE GETTING GREEDY, EXACTLY, BUT THEY WERE NOT FAR FROM IT. AT THE VERY LEAST, THEY WERE BEGINNING TO FEEL THEIR OATS—AND SERVED WITH PLENTY OF RICH CREAM THEY MADE A TASTY DISH. YES, SIR, THE BOYS WERE IN THE SADDLE, AND THEY THOUGHT THAT NOTHING COULD STOP THEM. BUT A FEW HUNDRED YEARS AGO A WISE OLD PHILOSOPHER MADE A VERY WONDERFUL REMARK—ONE THAT WE SHOULD ALWAYS REMEMBER. HE SAID: "JOE, YOU NEVER CAN TELL."

Scene 2

Back to MRS. PARTRIDGE'S *office.*

MISS SHOTGRAVEN *and* JENKINS *are locked in a long, long embrace. You could definitely say they like each other.*

As MRS. PARTRIDGE *enters they spring apart.*

JENKINS

Oh!

(He darts out.)

MISS SHOTGRAVEN
(Pulling herself together as well as she can)
I'm sorry, Mrs. Partridge. I promise you it won't happen again.

MRS. PARTRIDGE

Why not, darling?

MISS SHOTGRAVEN
(Trying to be businesslike)
The telephone has been ringing steadily. You have a great many messages.

MRS. PARTRIDGE

More? . . . Those terrible headlines! Weren't they wonderful?

MISS SHOTGRAVEN

Life magazine called up, and *Look,* and *Sensible Sex Weekly*. I don't know what *they* wanted.

MRS. PARTRIDGE

Pictures, probably. Send everyone who wants a picture to Vandamm. They took some lovely ones of me in 1926.

MISS SHOTGRAVEN

And several television producers, and—a lot of agents. I couldn't find out what they were agents *for*.

MRS. PARTRIDGE

Flesh, dear. Just flesh.

MISS SHOTGRAVEN

I beg your pardon?

MRS. PARTRIDGE

It's been a long time, Miss Shotgraven, since *they* called *me*. . . . Of course, it all comes a little late. . . . Don't let life go past you, Miss Shotgraven. Jump aboard it while you're young.

MISS SHOTGRAVEN
(*On the edge of tears*)
Oh, Mrs. Partridge, if I only could!

MRS. PARTRIDGE

Why, Amelia, darling, what's the matter?
(*But* MISS SHOTGRAVEN *just bursts into tears*)
Sit down here.

(*An arm around her*)
Now tell me what it is.
    (*More tears*)
Are you in trouble?
    (*Fresh tears*)
Bad trouble? . . . Who's the man?
    (MISS SHOTGRAVEN *gestures vaguely*)
Mark? It's all my fault. You were so unattractive with
your hair the other way. And now see what's happened!
. . . I suppose it wouldn't help now to put your hair
back again.
    (*Tears again*)
Have you told him?

MISS SHOTGRAVEN

Told him what?

MRS. PARTRIDGE

About your condition?

MISS SHOTGRAVEN

What condition?

MRS. PARTRIDGE

Then you're not going to—I mean, you aren't—

MISS SHOTGRAVEN

Of course not! How could you think such a thing?

MRS. PARTRIDGE

Well, in my day, when a girl said she was in trouble—
she was in trouble.

MISS SHOTGRAVEN

We can't afford to get married. He has to support his mother and sister, and I don't want to live with them.

MRS. PARTRIDGE

It *would* be crowded, wouldn't it?
(*More tears, broken by the entrance of* MR. SNELL.)

SNELL

Well, well! Good afternoon, Mrs. Partridge.

MISS SHOTGRAVEN

Excuse me, please.
(*She hurries out.*)

SNELL

(*Looking after her*)
Something wrong?

MRS. PARTRIDGE

Cinders. Both eyes.

SNELL

(*Squaring off*)
Mrs. Partridge, when is your birthday?

MRS. PARTRIDGE

Oh, Mr. Snell, you don't have to give me anything.

SNELL

It so happens, Mrs. Partridge, that the stockholders' meeting has been changed to the 14th of the month. And on the 14th, Mrs. Partridge, Saggitarius will be in the ascendency for those born under the Lion. You realize what that means.

MRS. PARTRIDGE

Oh! You're talking about my horoscope.

SNELL

Yes, Mrs. Partridge. It will be a very bad day for you to go out.

MRS. PARTRIDGE

Oh, you don't expect me to go by *that* damned nonsense.

SNELL

(*Somewhat stunned*)
You—don't believe in astrology?

MRS. PARTRIDGE

Not for stockholders' meetings.

SNELL

I see.
(*It needs a new attack*)
Mrs. Partridge, I wonder if you realize the position in which you have placed us.

MRS. PARTRIDGE

I'm terribly sorry.

SNELL

You were sent to Washington, Mrs. Partridge, to persuade Mr. McKeever to revise his attitude toward this company. Instead, you brought Mr. McKeever back to New York.

MRS. PARTRIDGE

But he was so unhappy there. He was a nervous wreck—you should have seen him.

SNELL

We want to protect you, Mrs. Partridge. We are very fond of you here at General Products.

MRS. PARTRIDGE

Oh, Mr. Snell.

SNELL

So we don't want you to feel that you *must* attend the forthcoming stockholders' meeting. You would be stared at, whispered about. We don't want you to be embarrassed.

MRS. PARTRIDGE

Oh, I'd like it.

SNELL

So to spare your feelings, Mrs. Partridge, we are prepared to buy your stock in the company. You're a good business woman. What would you say to five thousand dollars? That would be seventeen points over the market value.

MRS. PARTRIDGE

Seventeen? That's my lucky number. I signed for the best part I ever had on the 17th. It was in 1917, and the play ran for 17 months.

SNELL

Fine! Now if you'll just sign this form, transferring the
stock to us, you can bring the certificate in tomorrow.
And here is our check for $5,000.

MRS. PARTRIDGE

Oh, I want more than that if I'm going to be bribed,
Mr. Snell.

SNELL

Bribed! Who said anything about being bribed?

MRS. PARTRIDGE

You did. Why, when I show this to the other stockholders—

SNELL

Show what to the other stockholders?
    (*He is stuffing the paper and check into his
    pocket*)
May I remind you, Mrs. Partridge, that you have no
witnesses?
    (*And* MC KEEVER *enters.*)

MC KEEVER

Hope I'm not interrupting business.

MRS. PARTRIDGE

Oh, good afternoon, Mr. McKeever.

SNELL

Excuse me, Old-timer.
    (*And he goes.*)

MC KEEVER

Old-timer! In the Klondike I would have killed a man for that.

MRS. PARTRIDGE

Klondike! Did you ever see *Belle of the Klondike?*

MC KEEVER

I didn't see any women in the Klondike. I went there for gold. Dug for it with my bare hands.

MRS. PARTRIDGE

Mercy! Did you get any?

MC KEEVER

(*Shakes his head*)

Fellows with shovels were ahead of me. That's where I learned my first lesson: the little man doesn't stand a chance. But the trip was worth it. I met Robert W. Service.

(*This reminds him, and at once he goes into* "The Shooting of Dan McGrew," *with gestures*)

"A bunch of the boys were whooping it up in the Malamute Saloon"—

MRS. PARTRIDGE

(*Hastily*)

Yes, yes. . . . And after the Klondike?

MC KEEVER

Johannesburg. Diamonds. But the more I knocked around the more I realized: can't get ahead being a little fellow. Got to be big. So I came home. Worked my way back as a common seaman—

(*Stiffens up*)
lashed to the mast for seventy-two hours—typhoon.

MRS. PARTRIDGE

Gracious!

MC KEEVER

Landed in Frisco—started my own business.

MRS. PARTRIDGE

At last!

MC KEEVER

Lumber. Six months later they broke me. The Trust!

MRS. PARTRIDGE

Wasn't that mean of them?

MC KEEVER

No. It was business. Big business. So I made up my mind
then and there. Looked around for the biggest outfit I
could find and went to work at the bottom of the pile.

MRS. PARTRIDGE

The slag pile. I remember.

MC KEEVER

Old-timer! I should have fired him fifteen years ago,
when I caught him taking paper clips home. So what
happened? I'm out and they're in! And why? Because
I sold my stock. There's the goddam Senate for you
again!

MRS. PARTRIDGE

You've got to do something, Mr. McKeever.

MC KEEVER

Thirty-nine years with this company. When I went to Washington they gave me a gold key to this building. It's about all I have left.

MRS. PARTRIDGE

There'll be no dividends at all, with those men running things! Think of the stockholders!

MC KEEVER

Are you a stockholder?

MRS. PARTRIDGE

Ten shares.

MC KEEVER

Do you want my help?

MRS. PARTRIDGE

Oh, yes, Mr. McKeever!

MC KEEVER

You've got it!
    (*He weighs the situation*)
Now to get *them* out and take this company over again.

MRS. PARTRIDGE

    (*Encouragingly*)
That's it!

MC KEEVER

First time was easy. But these boys are smart—that's the
reason I put 'em *in* there. . . .
(*Thinking hard*)
Must be a way. All's fair in war and business, and by
God! This is both!

MRS. PARTRIDGE

I only wish I could help.

MC KEEVER
(*The glimmer of an idea*)
Maybe you can.

MRS. PARTRIDGE

I'll do anything!

MC KEEVER

Tell me. When they sent you down to Washington—
(*He stops, thoughtfully.*)

MRS. PARTRIDGE

Yes?
(*He is still thinking*)
What is it?

MC KEEVER

They *did* send you down to Washington, *didn't* they?

MRS. PARTRIDGE

Yes!

MC KEEVER

(*An edge of excitement in his voice*)
They bought your railroad ticket, and they had you met
at the station, and they delivered you to my office!

MRS. PARTRIDGE

Yes, they did.

MC KEEVER

To get Government contracts! Contracts for General
Products!

MRS. PARTRIDGE

(*Catching a little of his excitement*)
Yes!

MC KEEVER

Will you testify to that? Will you testify to that in court?

MRS. PARTRIDGE

Of course!

MC KEEVER

Then we've got them! There just happens to be a law
against that, Mrs. Partridge! A Federal law!

MRS. PARTRIDGE

(*A flash of divination*)
I know! The Mann Act!
(*And that's that.*)

Scene 3

Again the television screen.
A bell rings.

A VOICE

The six o'clock news round up, Bill Parker reporting.

PARKER

Good evening, ladies and gentlemen. First a look at the top story of the day—the United States Government versus General Products, Incorporated.

(*Shot of* LAURA *and* ED MC KEEVER *ascending the courthouse steps. They are both smiling and happy, and nod gayly to passers-by.*)

PARKER

(*His voice heard over the film clip*)

Up the steps of the Federal Courthouse in New York's Foley Square this morning went Mrs. Laura Partridge, key witness for the Government. Her purpose: to testify against directors of the mammoth General Products Corporation, charged with violation of the Smith-Wadsworth Anti-Lobbying Act. With her went businessman Edward L. McKeever, former Washington department head, who, the Government charged, was pressured by General Products directors. . . . A little later Clifford Snell, treasurer of General Products, and one of the accused men gives a statement to our television reporter. (*We see* SNELL, *in a corner of the building, lighting a cigarette, talking to a reporter, microphone in hand*)

SNELL

Mrs. Partridge's testimony is completely untrue. The decision to seek contracts in Washington was entirely her own. Speaking for the directors of General Products, we did not even know that she had gone to Washington until we read about it in the newspapers.

(*And now we go to* DWIGHT BROOKFIELD *and the second newsroom, used in Act. I.*)

BROOKFIELD

A very good evening, ladies and gentlemen. This is Dwight Brookfield bringing the eleven o'clock news right into your own living room. At exactly four-thirty this afternoon, the Government's case against one of the nation's largest corporations came to an abrupt end. A federal jury refused to convict the corporation's directors, and instead severely censured Mrs. Laura Partridge, the Government's chief witness. Subsequently, Federal Judge Manson J. Madison also criticized Mrs. Partridge's action, declaring that as a stockholder in General Products she stood to profit by influencing a government employee in its favor.

(LAURA *and* ED MC KEEVER *are shown coming down the courthouse steps. They have newspapers over their heads to thwart the photographers, and are plainly trying to evade questioning reporters. As the reporters become more importunate they*

*quicken their steps, finally breaking into a run.
At the foot of the steps they find a taxi—reporters
crowding close.)*

The Narrator

SO CINDERELLA WENT AWAY FROM THERE, CLOSELY FOL-
LOWED BY REPRESENTATIVES OF THE TIMES, THE TRIBUNE,
THE NEWS, THE MIRROR, THE POST, THE JOURNAL, THE
WORLD-TELEGRAM, AND WOMEN'S WEAR. AND THIS SHOULD
TEACH EVERYONE A GREAT LESSON. WHENEVER YOU SEE A
LAWYER, ANYWHERE, RUN LIKE HELL.

Scene 4

The big office.
The unholy quartet are ranged behind the desk
this time. And it is MRS. PARTRIDGE *who is sitting*
nervously before them.

SNELL

So under the circumstances, Mrs. Partridge, I'm afraid
that's the way it will have to be.

MRS. PARTRIDGE

You're angry because I testified for the other side. That's
why you're discharging me.

BLESSINGTON

(*Not very convincing*)
Why, not at all, Mrs. Partridge!

GILLIE

Not at all!

SNELL

(*Unctuous*)
Nothing could be further from our minds.

MRS. PARTRIDGE

Hasn't my work been satisfactory?

BLESSINGTON

Yes, indeed. Very much so.

MRS. PARTRIDGE

Letters are coming in every day, hundreds of them.

METCALFE

We know that, Mrs. Partridge.

MRS. PARTRIDGE

If it's another retrenchment move, I'd be willing to take a slight cut.

SNELL

I'm afraid not.

MRS. PARTRIDGE

Say a hundred dollars. Just because I like the work.

SNELL

No, no.

MRS. PARTRIDGE

Eighty-five? That's Equity minimum.

SNELL

The cashier has your check waiting for you, Mrs. Partridge, terminating your employment as of this afternoon.
(*Rising*)
And now if you will excuse us—

MRS. PARTRIDGE

Of course. . . . No one wants to say anything else?
        (*There is silence*)
Well, I do. . . . The way you men are running things,
I wouldn't be surprised if this company closes on Satur-
day night.
        (*And she goes.*)

BLESSINGTON

What did she mean by that?

SNELL

What's the difference what she says? There's nothing she
can do any more.

GILLIE

I'm kind of worried about it.

BLESSINGTON

She might still show up at the meeting—queer everything.

SNELL

Not a chance! After the way the judge laced into her?
Nobody would listen to a word she said. . . . No, sir,
we're in the clear. Forget about that grouse woman—
we're going to have our biggest year.

METCALFE

We are?

SNELL

You bet we are! With McKeever out of Washington we're starting to get Government contracts again.

BLESSINGTON

And *are* we soaking them! You know those ten million filing cabinets we got stuck with last year?

GILLIE

Yes?

BLESSINGTON

Well, we pressed them down flat and sold 'em to the Government for fences.

METCALFE

What's the Government want with all those fences?

BLESSINGTON

Indians. You can't let 'em run around, can you?

SNELL

Yes, sir, our biggest year! And, gentlemen, *no excess profits tax.*

GILLIE

Why not?

SNELL

Because there isn't any any more.

GILLIE

Oh, I thought maybe we just weren't going to pay it.

SNELL

Anybody want a drink?

BLESSINGTON

I wish you fellows would bring a bottle of your own in here some day. My expense account is beginning to look outrageous.

SNELL

$1155 last month. I checked it myself.

BLESSINGTON

Who told you to stick your nose into my business?

SNELL

I'm Treasurer, you know. . . . Say, *we* didn't drink all that whiskey, did we?

BLESSINGTON

It wasn't just whiskey—there were other things.
  (*His watch*)
Four-thirty. . . . Would you fellows mind taking your drinks and drifting into one of the other offices?

METCALFE

Not going to work, are you, Jack?

BLESSINGTON

  (*The phone*)
Miss Condon. I forgot. Get my home—tell Mrs. Blessington I've got to stay in town tonight.

128

SNELL

(*Raising his glass*)
Well, boys! Here's to General Products! And to us!

GILLIE

You're sure nothing can happen? I'm still a little nervous.

SNELL

Relax, Warren—She's probably got her check and is out
of the building by this time.
(*His glass on high again*)
To General Products!

BLESSINGTON

General Products!

GILLIE

General Products!
(*And* MC KEEVER *stalks in*)
(*There is a chorus of greeting: "How do you do,
Mr. McKeever." "Ed!" "Hello, Ed!"*)

MC KEEVER

(*Not even a curt nod. Takes off his coat and throws
it onto a chair*)
On your feet, goddam it! All of you!

GILLIE

(*Placatingly*)
Now look here, Mr. McKeever—

METCALFE

What the hell's the matter with you, Ed?

SNELL

Take it easy, McKeever. You'll get ulcers.

MC KEEVER

I don't *get* ulcers. I *give* 'em.

SNELL

What kind of grandstand play is this?

MC KEEVER

I want you to give that woman her job back.

BLESSINGTON

My dear fellow!

METCALFE

Is *that* all?

BLESSINGTON

The way you steamed in here, one would have thought it was something important.

MC KEEVER

It's important to *me*.

SNELL

May I ask why?

MC KEEVER

Because she loves that job, and I want her to have it back.

GILLIE

Of course, Mr. McKeever.

SNELL

Well! We'd like to help you, McKeever. But it puts us in rather an untenable position. She's been dismissed—severance papers sent through half an hour ago. You know your own policy—never rescind an order.

MC KEEVER

I don't give a damn about details. I want her back.

SNELL

You don't mean to say that the great Ed McKeever came in here just to ask for an old lady's job?

MC KEEVER

I know what's eating you. The trial. That wasn't her doing. It was mine.

SNELI

Then how do you have the gall to come here and ask a favor!

BLESSINGTON

Something in what he says, Ed—when you come to think of it.

GILLIE

Fair's fair, you know, Mr. McKeever.

MC KEEVER

I'm just telling you to give that woman her job back.

SNELL
(*Entirely too quietly*)
You're not telling us anything.

MC KEEVER
Yes, yes. These are your offices now, aren't they? Not mine. You're running the company, not me.

SNELL
And don't get the idea you can do anything about it.

BLESSINGTON
He's right, Ed. Be sensible. We've got control, the four of us.

METCALFE
For old times' sake, Ed, I don't like to see you make a fool of yourself.

BLESSINGTON
Take my advice, Ed—don't make an issue of it.

MC KEEVER
Are you boys trying to tell me the financial setup of my own company?

SNELL
Our company.

MC KEEVER
My mistake.

SNELL

Times have changed, McKeever. And you're getting a little old.

MC KEEVER

Why, you miserable—

BLESSINGTON

Now hold on, Ed! Clifford's worked extremely hard for this company. We all have. It's all we've had our minds on, day and night.
(*And right on cue* MISS L'ARRIERE *enters. Mink coat, everything*)

MISS L'ARRIERE

Honest to God, Jack, aren't you ever coming?—Oh, I didn't know you had a meeting, Mr. Blessington. Excuse me.
(*And she tiptoes out.*)

MC KEEVER

(*Enjoying himself hugely*)
Day and night, eh?

BLESSINGTON

I don't know what you're talking about.

MC KEEVER

I'll tell you what I'm talking about. Ruthie. The girl downstairs in the cafeteria that made the chicken cro-quettes. And the girl in the shipping department who had to come up here to keep you informed about what kind of twine we were using. And the receptionist who got pains from sitting so long, you had to let her rest on your couch.

BLESSINGTON

Really!
(*As* SNELL *laughs*)
Clifford!

MC KEEVER

Yes, I don't know what Snell's laughing about. Did I ever tell you boys about the night he got stuck in the transom, trying to sneak into my office? I never did find out what you were after that night, Snell. What was it?

SNELL
(*Pretty mean, by this time*)
There's nothing here for you any more, McKeever. You're through. So why don't you get the hell out?

MC KEEVER
(*Looks at each one in turn. They fail to meet his eye. He takes the gold key from his pocket*)
Thirty-nine years. Well, I don't need a key to get out.
(*Tosses the key onto the desk, turns and goes*)
(*Pretty tense, we can tell you.*)

The Narrator

WELL! THINGS LOOKED PRETTY BLACK FOR CINDERELLA AND PRINCE CHARMING, I CAN TELL YOU THAT. NOT ONLY WAS THE GLASS SLIPPER LOST, IT WAS BROKEN IN A THOUSAND PIECES. YOU PROBABLY THINK THAT VIRTUE IS NOT GOING TO BE REWARDED. BUT DON'T GIVE UP YET, BECAUSE IF CINDERELLA DOES NOT WIND UP HAPPY, WE WILL GIVE ALL YOU YOUR MONEY BACK. AND THERE IS A FAT CHANCE OF THAT.

Scene 5

LAURA PARTRIDGE's *office.*

MRS. PARTRIDGE, *having been fired, is cleaning out her desk.*

This is equivalent to a woman emptying out her handbag, but on a large scale. The things that come out of MRS. PARTRIDGE's *desk are quaint indeed, and yet rather to be expected:*

(*A sheaf of papers*)

(*A red galosh. But no second one, though she searches high and low*)

(*A coffee pot*)

(*A cup and saucer*)

(*A piggy bank*)

(*A box of Lux*)

(*A fan*)

(*A mirror*)

(*An umbrella*)

(*An empty milk bottle*)

(*A pair of nylons*)

(*A raincoat*)

(*A hot-water bottle*)

(*The second galosh, at last. From somewhere in the bookcase*)

(*A girdle, from the filing cabinet*)

(*She busily stows all these things into a great brief case, then fishes up an old* Variety *from a*

bottom drawer and settles down happily to read)
(At which point MR. MC KEEVER *strides in.)*

MRS. PARTRIDGE

Oh, Mr. McKeever! . . . Goodness. Imagine your walking in on me like this. This place must look a mess. I'm packing.

MC KEEVER

Yes, I know. And I'm burning mad.

MRS. PARTRIDGE

Nonsense. You mustn't feel that way. I'm glad.

MC KEEVER

Glad that I didn't get you your job back?

MRS. PARTRIDGE

Glad that I was here. Because if I hadn't been I never would have learned about second breakfasts and things like that. Oh, well. There's no business like business.

(GILLIE *and* SNELL *stroll in.*)

SNELL

Now, my idea, Gillie . . .
    (*He sees* MC KEEVER)
Oh, still here? . . . My idea is to put shelves in here—wall to wall. Floor to ceiling.

GILLIE

Floor to ceiling. Very good.

SNELL

We're going to use this room for dead storage. You see, we're putting in a whole new system. Modern.
(*To* MC KEEVER. *Right to* MC KEEVER)
Because once something is over and finished with, Mc-Keever, it's better to get it out of the way.
(*He turns back to* GILLIE)
And say listen, why don't we go down to the cellar? I'll bet we can find a spot down there for that bust.
(*A nasty look at* MC KEEVER, *and they go.*)

MC KEEVER

I wish I knew about seven new words.

MRS. PARTRIDGE

You'll beat them, Mr. McKeever. You're Aries the Ram. You're strong, forceful, determined.

MC KEEVER

Y'know, these past few weeks, Mrs. Partridge, I've got to know you pretty well. I hope you won't laugh at what I'm going to say.

MRS. PARTRIDGE

I never laugh at you, Mr. McKeever. Oh, you mean that recitation. That was the material, not you.

MC KEEVER

Anyhow, dropping in here every few days the way I've

been doing, I've read some of those letters you've been sending out. And I read some of the answers you got from the stockholders, too. . . . Mrs. Partridge, I'll come right to the point. I'm going back into business. What would you think of joining me?

MRS. PARTRIDGE

Oh, I'm not a business woman. Anyhow, not a real one. I haven't done so well here at General Products.

MC KEEVER

Forget about General Products. It's big, but there's room for more than one big show in this town.

MRS. PARTRIDGE

Oh, there certainly is! Why, when the Hippodrome opened . . .

MC KEEVER

Yes. . . . Then what do you say? We could sound a whole new note in industry.

MRS. PARTRIDGE

Well, I don't know.

MC KEEVER

Edward L. McKeever & Company.

MRS. PARTRIDGE

What?

MC KEEVER

Edward L. McKeever & Company.

MRS. PARTRIDGE

Well, I never was a star, but in my last three plays . . . Couldn't it be Edward L. McKeever *with* Laura Partridge?

MC KEEVER

Anything you say. McKeever & Partridge.

MRS. PARTRIDGE

Equal billing. That's very generous . . . but I don't know. . . .

MC KEEVER

Only before we go any further, there's something I've got to tell you.

MRS. PARTRIDGE

Yes?

MC KEEVER

I never would have mentioned it if this hadn't come up.

MRS. PARTRIDGE

What is it, Mr. McKeever?

MC KEEVER

It's something you ought to know. I hope it won't disturb you too much.

MRS. PARTRIDGE

You can tell me anything, Mr. McKeever. Anything.

MC KEEVER

(*Hangs his head*)
I've only got fifteen million dollars.
(*Looks up with a brave smile*)
But I've got a group of men behind me who'll come in on
anything if I give the word.

MRS. PARTRIDGE

(*She can understand* this)
You mean you've got backers, too?

MC KEEVER

I guess that's what you call them.

MRS. PARTRIDGE

Well, with all that money, what would you think of starting a little repertory theatre?

MC KEEVER

Theatre?

MRS. PARTRIDGE

Repertory. That means doing a different play every night.
Just good plays, you understand. I think it's the very thing
New York wants.

MC KEEVER

A theatre, eh? Might be something in *that,* too. Would
you act in it?

MRS. PARTRIDGE

Well, I could. Maybe some of the old Sarah Bernhardt
plays. They had wonderful women's parts in them.

MC KEEVER

Ye-es. . . . What are the men's parts like in those shows?

MRS. PARTRIDGE

(*Oh, no!*)
On second thought, Mr. McKeever, I don't think New York is ready for repertory.

MC KEEVER

I wouldn't expect to play big parts—at least not right away.

MRS. PARTRIDGE

(*Firmly*)
No, Mr. McKeever. I'm afraid we'd better forget that kind of partnership.

MC KEEVER

And you're sure you don't want to go into business with me?

MRS. PARTRIDGE

You're being very kind, Mr. McKeever, but it's a little late for me to start studying new lines.

MC KEEVER

Is there anything I can do for you? Anything at all?
(MRS. PARTRIDGE *shakes her head, smiles*)
Well—what are you going to do?

MRS. PARTRIDGE

Oh, I've made arrangements. I'm going into the Actor's Fund Home.

MC KEEVER

Actors Home? I couldn't let you do that.

MRS. PARTRIDGE

Oh, it's not like it sounds. You're perfectly independent there, and there are other actors and actresses, and lots of talk about show business. I'm signing over my ten shares of stock to them, but the dividends will be mine, as long as I live.

MC KEEVER

I see.

MRS. PARTRIDGE

If you'd like to, you can visit me sometimes. Englewood isn't a very long drive—with that big car of yours and the chauffeur. You will drive out, won't you, Mr. Mc-Keever? My, that will impress those old character women, all right. . . . Well, I've got to be getting these things together.

(*Picks up letters*)

All of these people that have been writing to me. I'm taking some of their letters home to answer—I really feel that they've sort of become friends.

MC KEEVER

Where'd you get this?

(*Picking up a little green slip of paper*)

MRS. PARTRIDGE

It must have been in this letter. (*Looks at it*)

Yes. . . . Mrs. Weaver.

(*She reads*)

"Enclosed please find photograph of Harold. It was taken last summer in the back yard next to the garage. Am also inclosing my proxy for the next stockholders' meeting."

. . . Is that a proxy?

MC KEEVER

Yes, it is.

MRS. PARTRIDGE

(*Continues to read*)

"I generally don't bother sending them back, but since you and I have been corresponding I feel much closer to the company. So I wrote your name in the blank space, because you are the only one at General Products I'm acquainted with. I hope it arrives in time."

(*She looks again at the proxy*)

Thirty shares.

MC KEEVER

(*Delving into her pile of papers*)

Here's another one. Fifty shares.

(*Reads from the accompanying letter*)

"I am sending this to you because I feel that you have my interests at heart. I know that you will cast my vote for the best man there."

MRS. PARTRIDGE

My goodness, I don't know what to do with these. Do you, Mr. McKeever?

(MC KEEVER *nods sagely. At which point* MARK JENKINS *enters, pushing a small truck loaded to the gills with mail.* JENKINS *is pretty well mussed up—collar open, shirt torn. He is followed by an agitated* MISS SHOTGRAVEN.)

JENKINS

Well, I made it.

MRS. PARTRIDGE

Mark Jenkins! What's happened to you?

MISS SHOTGRAVEN

He's been fired! That's what's happened. A fist fight with Mr. Snell.

JENKINS

Laid him out cold, if you must know.

MC KEEVER

You did? Oh, that's too bad.

MRS. PARTRIDGE

But why?

JENKINS

He didn't want me to make this delivery.

MISS SHOTGRAVEN

Oh, Mark! *Now* what are we going to do?

JENKINS

I tell you, Mrs. Partridge, ever since I've been in the mail room, we've never had a flood like this.

MRS. PARTRIDGE

(*Picking up a letter*)

It's another one of those proxy papers. Mercy! Two hundred shares.

MISS SHOTGRAVEN

Fifty-five shares!

MC KEEVER

A hundred and sixty!

MISS SHOTGRAVEN

Mark, close the door!

MC KEEVER

Three hundred shares! Mark, lock the door!

(*But* SNELL *and* BLESSINGTON *have entered, full steam ahead.*)

SNELL

(*To* BLESSINGTON)

Here you are! See for yourself! You and that damned letter writing you put her up to!

BLESSINGTON

Just a moment, Mrs. Partridge! What is the meaning of this!
(*To* SNELL)
You're sure these are all proxies?

SNELL

Of course, I'm sure!
(*To* MRS. PARTRIDGE)
You're not working for General Products any more, Mrs. Partridge! These are company property!

MRS. PARTRIDGE

Goodness! Well, I don't want any trouble.

MC KEEVER

Pardon me, gentlemen! These belong to Mrs. Partridge, all of them. Her name is on every one.

SNELL

That doesn't matter! A mere handful! We've got more than that up in the office.

JENKINS

No, you haven't, Mr. Snell! There are five thousand letters here, and twice as many down in the mail room. All you've got is about three hundred.

(MC KEEVER *starts digging in the cart.*)

SNELL

Shut up, Jenkins! You've been discharged too!

(METCALFE *and* GILLIE *come hurrying in.*)

METCALFE

So this is where you are!

GILLIE

Why weren't we told about this?

SNELL

Oh, shut up, Gillie. I can lick *you*!

MC KEEVER

Five thousand letters! And they average about two hundred shares.

MRS. PARTRIDGE

(*Beaming*)
Aren't they the darlingest people?

MC KEEVER

You don't realize it, Mrs. Partridge, but you're in control of this entire company.

MRS. PARTRIDGE

I am?

MC KEEVER

You certainly are!

SNELL

But that's purely technical, you understand, Mrs. Partridge.

MRS. PARTRIDGE

Goodness, I understand! I've learned about business. Well—This means just one thing. Gentlemen, you're all fired.

(*Everyone enjoys it except our four villains.*)

The Narrator

AND SO, A FEW DAYS LATER, ARM IN ARM WITH PRINCE
CHARMING, CINDERELLA MADE ANOTHER TRIP DOWNTOWN.
ONLY THIS TIME, NOT IN THE SUBWAY, NOT IN A COACH
DRAWN BY SIX WHITE HORSES, BUT IN A SOLID GOLD CADIL-
LAC, DRIVEN BY A SOLID GOLD CHAUFFEUR.

Scene 6

The stockholders' meeting.

ED MC KEEVER *and* LAURA *behind the big table—*
MISS SHOTGRAVEN *at the side, busily taking notes.*
And no *one else.*

MRS. PARTRIDGE
(*On her feet, and obviously just finishing her con-*
tribution to the proceedings)
Respectfully submitted, at this, the sixtieth annual meet-
ing of General Products, Incorporated. . . . Signed,
Laura Partridge, Vice-President, Secretary and Treasurer.

MC KEEVER
You have heard the report of the Vice-President, Secretary and Treasurer. Those in favor say aye.

(JENKINS *brings on a great wire basket, filled with*
proxies)
MRS. PARTRIDGE
(*Blandly*)
Voting 17 million shares by proxy, I say Aye.
(*The old lucky number*)

MC KEEVER
All opposed? . . . Motion carried!

150

(*But a little old lady gets to her feet.*)
Yes, Madam?

OLD LADY

Excuse me. May I ask a question?

MRS. PARTRIDGE

Oh, no! That's how I got *my* start!
(*She grabs the gavel and starts banging*)
The meeting is adjourned! The meeting is adjourned!

And the Final Curtain Falls